TWO
SHAKESPEAREAN
ACTORS

RICHARD NELSON

faber and faber
LONDON · BOSTON

For Anton Lesser and Roger Michell

Photoset by Parker Typesetting Service Leicester

Printed in the United States of America

This play concerns imagined events surrounding the following true incident: on Thursday 10 May 1849, while the English actor William Charles Macready was performing *Macbeth* at the Astor Place Opera House in New York City, a riot erupted which resulted in the death of thirty-four people and the injury of over a hundred more.

Two Shakespearean Actors opened at the Swan Theatre, Stratford-upon-Avon, on 29 August 1990. The cast was as follows:

MRS CATHERINE FORREST	Mary Chater
MRS POPE	Penny Jones
MISS JANE BASS	Polly Kemp
MRS AGNES BOUCICAULT	Yolanda Vazquez
MISS HELEN BURTON	Catherine White
THOMAS FISHER	George Anton
WASHINGTON IRVING	John Bott
JOHN SEFTON	Michael Bott
FREDERICK WEMYSS	Alfred Burke
CHARLES CLARK	Michael Gardiner
DION BOUCICAULT	Ciaran Hinds
JOHN RYDER	Paul Jesson
EDWIN FORREST	Anton Lesser
SCOTT	Trevor Martin
TILTON	George Raistrick
JAMES BRIDGES	Vincent Regan
ROBERT JONES	Ken Shorter
GEORGE BRADSHAW	John Warnaby
WILLIAM CHARLES MACREADY	John Carlisle
MR BLAKELY	Arnold Yarrow
MISS ANN HOLLAND	Georgiana Dacombe
PETER ARNOLD	Andrew Havill
MR CHIPPINDALE	Bill McGuirk
Director	Roger Michell
Assistant Director	Clarissa Brown
Designer	Alexander Byrne
Lighting Designer	Rick Fisher
Music	Jeremy Sams
Stage Management	Jondon Gourkan
	David Mann
	Liz Lawrence

CHARACTERS

Actors at the Broadway Theatre (in parenthesis, the parts they play)
EDWIN FORREST (Macbeth; Metamora), early forties
MISS JANE BASS (1st Witch), twenties
MISS HELEN BURTON (2nd Witch; Goodenough), twenties
MISS ANNE HOLLAND (3rd Witch; Nahmeokee), twenties
TILTON (Porter; Church), sixties
THOMAS FISHER (Young Siward; Kaweshine), late twenties
FANNY WALLACK (Lady Macbeth), forties
ROBERT JONES (Banquo, Malcolm; Anrawandah), early thirties
MR BLAKELY (Duncan; Errington), fifties
SCOTT (who normally plays Macduff, but is injured), thirties
JOHN RYDER (who fills in as Macduff), English and the travelling
    companion of Macready, thirties.

*Actors at the Astor Place Opera House (in parenthesis, the parts they
play)*
WILLIAM CHARLES MACREADY (Macbeth), English, late fifties
CHARLES CLARK (Macduff), forties
MRS POPE (Lady Macbeth), thirties
GEORGE BRADSHAW (Banquo), forties
FREDERICK WEMYSS (Siward, Old Man), sixties
JAMES BRIDGES (Young Siward, 3rd Witch, Ross), early twenties
JOHN SEFTON (1st Witch, Donalbain), forties
MR CHIPPINDALE (2nd Witch), forties
PETER ARNOLD (Malcolm), twenties

Others
CATHERINE FORREST, wife of Edwin, English, thirties
MISS WEMYSS, an aspiring actress, daughter of Frederick
    Wemyss, late teens
DION BOUCICAULT, playwright and actor, English/Irish, thirties
AGNES ROBERTSON, actress and Boucicault's wife, late twenties
WASHINGTON IRVING, writer and amateur actor, sixties
Other actors, and servants

ACT ONE

SCENE I

Projection: Thursday 3 May 1849. 11 p.m.

A tavern, New York.

    Two large tables. At one table: six men and two women –
WILLIAM CHARLES MACREADY, JOHN RYDER, CHARLES CLARK,
GEORGE BRADSHAW, JAMES BRIDGES, FREDERICK WEMYSS, *and*
MRS POPE, *and* MISS WEMYSS. *With the exceptions of* MISS
WEMYSS *and* JOHN RYDER, *all are members of Macready's acting
company, that is now rehearsing a production of* Macbeth *at the Astor
Place Opera House.*

    At the other table: TILTON, *an older actor, who is a member of the
acting company Edwin Forrest is now performing with at the
Broadway Theatre.*

    The MACREADY *group has been here for some time; beer, wine, etc.
on the table.* TILTON *has only just arrived.*

CLARK: (*To* TILTON *as he sits down*) How did it happen?
BRADSHAW: Before you answer that, who was he playing?
TILTON: Cassio.
    (*Beat.*)
BRADSHAW: Scott as Cassio? I thought he was Forrest's Iago?
MRS POPE: Not this season. (*Beat.*)
    Earlier in the season.
TILTON: Who told you that?
MRS POPE: In Baltimore wasn't he Iago?
TILTON: Scott told you that.
MRS POPE: Didn't he sit here, at this very table and say he was
    born to play Iago? (*Beat.*) I heard him say this. Did anyone
    else hear him say this? (*Beat.*) He said this is what he learned
    from playing the part in Baltimore. Or maybe it was
    Philadelphia.
TILTON: He's never played Iago in his life. (*Beat.*) Once he
    played it. Something like five people had to get sick at the
    same time. It took that sort of luck. And then he knew about

I

every third line. That's not playing Iago. (*Beat.*) He's never actually played the part.

MRS POPE: You played Iago, didn't you, Tilton?

TILTON: For years and years.

(*Short pause.*)

Anyway, he slipped. Playing Cassio he slipped. And . . . (*Beat.*) I wasn't on stage. This is what everyone was telling me.

CLARK: How much of the finger did he cut off?

TILTON: All of it! (*Beat.*) I don't know. There was blood everywhere, though. I saw his shirt. After he left, it was there lying across a chair. (*Beat.*) Blood all over it. (*Beat.*) Someone said the dagger cut it all off and it was still on stage. (*Beat.*) But I didn't see it. So . . . (*Shrugs.*)

(*Short pause.*)

BRADSHAW: What else was Scott playing, Tilton?

TILTON: Let me think. In *Jack Cade* – what? What does he play? (*Beat.*) I'm not in *Jack Cade*. I don't remember. (*Beat.*) He's very good in it, they say. (*Beat.*) But we don't do *Jack Cade* for – two weeks? I don't remember. I think that. And then there's his Macduff. He does play Macduff. I don't know what Ned'll do about losing a Macduff. There's a part I also used to play.

MRS POPE: I can see how that would have been a very good role for you.

TILTON: My wife always said that same thing. She loved my Macduff. (*Beat.*) I always thought that odd – for a wife to like such a part – what with all that happens to his family in the play.

MRS POPE: I doubt if she was thinking about it that way.

TILTON: She was a smart woman, Mrs Pope.

MRS POPE: I remember her well.

(*Beat.*)

RYDER: (*Suddenly stands and calls*) If you need a Macduff! If this – . If he – .

(*Others look at him.*)

I know the part. I've played . . . I'm not doing anything at this – . Now. (*Turns to* MACREADY) Unless you think – .

2

(*Beat.*)

CLARK: (*Introducing*) Mr John Ryder.

(TILTON *nods.*)

And Mr Macready, I'm sure you –

TILTON: I have seen you on stage many many times, sir.

(MACREADY *smiles, then turns to* RYDER.)

MACREADY: (*Nodding towards* TILTON) What's his – ?

(RYDER *shrugs.*)

MRS POPE: Tilton.

(MACREADY *shakes his head, not knowing who he is.*)

(*Short pause.*)

TILTON: I shall pass this information along to Mr Forrest.

RYDER: Thank you. I would appreciate it. (*Sits. Beat. Suddenly stands again.*) Would you care to join us? If that's all – .

TILTON: I am supposed to save – . (*Gestures 'this table'.*)

(RYDER *nods and sits. Pause.*)

BRADSHAW: I wonder how long he'll be out.

(*Beat.* MRS POPE *looks at him.*)

Scott.

WEMYSS: I wonder if he was drinking. Scott drinks.

MRS POPE: Not any more. Not like when he did drink.

WEMYSS: He was drinking like that last week.

MACREADY: (*Interrupting, not having listened to what anyone has been saying*) I only want to say – to all of you – that I am having a wonderful time. So thank you.

(*Others nod at him.*)

MRS POPE: (*To* WEMYSS) When did you see him last week?

MACREADY: (*Interrupting again*) I think our rehearsals . . . I want you to know I could not be more pleased. And I am not speaking as an Englishman to – . (*Beat.*) No, I happen to love American – . Everything here is so – . It's rich. It's – . I was telling John just the other day, wasn't it? I was saying that *I* think American accents, they are so much closer to what Shakespeare himself spoke. You are so much closer. I think this has almost been proven. I mean, you – as American actors – . I appreciate the way you have taken me in. The warmth. I feel this. I – . (*Beat.*) Thank you. (*Beat. Stares at* CLARK.) Much closer to what Shakespeare himself spoke!

3

You! Without even – . Just instinctively. All one's
sophistication it really can get in the way, can't it?! (*Laughs*.)
We poor English actors – right, John? Well, it's so much
hard work and practice and study, and then one comes here
and sees you – .How you – . The energy it comes so easy for
you.
(*Short pause. He looks at each actor at his table, one by one.*)
Anyway, I salute you. I have wanted to say this all week.
Every night I tell John, I meant to say this. Here I have
found in New York, an American group of – . Which is
almost like a group of English actors. I can't say more.
(*Short pause.*)
Let me get some more to drink. (*Reaches for money.*) I won't
stay long, I promise you. Don't worry. (*Laughs to himself.*) I
want to buy – . I want to pay. (*Takes out money, turns to*
RYDER.) John, would you . . .?
(*Hands money to* RYDER, *who hesitates.* MACREADY *drinks.*
RYDER *goes off to the bar. Pause.*)

WEMYSS: (*To* MRS POPE) Last week. Maybe Tuesday. He was in
here drinking like he used to.

MRS POPE: I'm sorry to hear that.

BRADSHAW: And after he slipped and cut himself – .

TILTON: Cut it off. The whole finger's off.

BRADSHAW: He then what? What happened to the – .

TILTON: They finished the scene. Everyone. Scott too. Like
nothing had happened. Blood was spurting and he stays.

MRS POPE: Incredible.

MACREADY: Good for him! Good for him!

MRS POPE: (*To herself, shaking her head*) For two dollars a
performance.

CLARK: Something like that happens, you don't think, you act
instinctively.

MRS POPE: Stupidly.

MACREADY: (*Bangs the table, ignoring everyone*) Good for him!
(*Laughs.*) John's like that too. My good friend John.
(*Gestures towards where* RYDER *left, then laughs.*) He was in
Spartacus. With me. This was with me in Leeds. (*Coughs,
getting everyone's attention.*) Listen to this. He needs to come

4

on with his arm on fire. And we have worked this out.
Carefully. (*Beat*.) His arm on fire. (*Beat*.) A metal band is
put around his arm. And he carries a blanket – so if anything
does happen . . . Which it shouldn't, but you want to be safe.
This is an actor that I employ. I must be safe. The blanket he
is to take and pat out the flame if – . Whatever. If he needs
to, has to. Anyway, he lights the flame just before his
entrance. And he comes on now. (*Beat*.) Fire blazing. Great
effect. But someone this time has missed a cue. So we wait a
moment. This happens even in the English theatre, let me
tell you. Someone misses an entrance. (*Beat*.) So the fire
blazes for a little longer than it is supposed to. But John, he
– . He does nothing. Then he leaves. And so on. But then
later we hear that his whole arm is quite badly burned.
(*Beat*.) He had let it burn! And why? Because he said – .
(*Beat*.) The line he is to speak – he has a line which normally
comes only a few seconds after he enters, but – and now this
line, because of the mistake, it's coming a bit later, he says it
– the line – I forget the line, but he says it. And it gets a nice
little laugh. It always gets a nice little laugh. (*Beat*.) And he
says, that's why he didn't want to pat out the fire. Because he
needed the blaze, he thought, to get that nice laugh. (*Beat*.)
So he let his arm burn!
(*Laughs. Short pause.*)
(*Adds*) Just to get the laugh!
MRS POPE: We understood.
(*No one else is laughing.*)
MACREADY: (*Laughing*) I love John. From that day, I have loved
him. That's the sort of – . I don't know. (*Beat*.) Nothing
deceptive about him. Very rare for an actor. (*Beat*.) A good
friend. (*Smiles*.) A good man to have around. (*Drinks*.)
(*Long pause.*)
TILTON: (*Finally*) Scott's wife was nearly hysterical. (*Beat*.) She's
pregnant.
BRADSHAW: (*To* MRS POPE) You know his wife.
(*She nods*.)
MACREADY: (*Suddenly hits the table again*) In England, acting is a
noble profession, gentlemen! (*Beat*.) And ladies.

5

(RYDER *enters with more to drink. No one says anything as he sets the drinks down. Awkward pause.*)
I won't ask you to show your scar, John.
(*Laughs.*)
MRS POPE: (*Quickly changing the subject*) Anyone else seen Hackett?
WEMYSS: Why would we – ?
MRS POPE: He's offering seasons. He offered me a season.
WEMYSS: I wouldn't take a season.
MRS POPE: He's doubled what he's paying. At least for me. (*Beat.*) I may take a season.
BRADSHAW: He never asks me. We socialize. My wife sees his wife. Two three times a month, I think. But he never . . .
TILTON: He came around last week after *Richelieu*.
MRS POPE: I heard this.
TILTON: He made offers. (*Beat.*) To Jack. To Mary. To Florence.
BRADSHAW: Why does he need both Mary *and* Florence?
WEMYSS: Which Jack? Wheatley?
TILTON: Hooper. Jack Hooper.
MRS POPE: Jack Wheatley's ill. Didn't you know?
WEMYSS: No. No, I didn't.
(*Beat.*)
BRADSHAW: I thought you'd worked a lot with Wheatley.
WEMYSS: No.
BRADSHAW: Weren't you together in – .
WEMYSS: Wheatley wasn't in it then. When I was. (*Beat.*) I took over his role. I saw him play the role. We've met. We've been out together. Many times. In groups. Nice man. (*Beat.*) He's not that old.
CLARK: He is a nice man.
BRIDGES: He has children everywhere.
MRS POPE: I've heard this.
WEMYSS: Where is he?
TILTON: At home. Went back to his wife.
(*Short pause.*)
WEMYSS: (*To his daughter*) We're about the same age. Wheatley and me.

6

MACREADY: (*Grabs* CLARK'*s shoulder*) Mr Clark, it was a very
good rehearsal today. Very good.
(*Beat.*)
CLARK: Thank you.
(*Short pause.*)
MRS POPE: Mr Macready, as you've brought up the rehearsals
. . . (*She looks at the others for a second.*) Do you happen to
know if I'll be needed tomorrow in the afternoon?
MACREADY: I don't know. (*Short pause.*) You have something else
to do.
MRS POPE: If I'm needed I will be there. (*Short pause.*) If I'm not
my sister has planned a tea – . She would like me to – . She
needs some help. (*Beat.*)
(*Turns to the others.*) But I wouldn't want to – . If it's a
bother. I can work all morning. Right through lunch if you
wish. If that would help.
MACREADY: I'll do what I can, Mrs Pope.
MRS POPE: I don't want it to be a problem, so if – . (*Turns to
others.*) If it's going to cause anyone any . . . (*Beat.*) Is it?
(*Beat.*) I guess it isn't, Mr Macready. No one said – .
MACREADY: I will do what I can, Mrs Pope.
(*Long pause. Only now does it become clear just how drunk*
MACREADY *is. He holds his head, breathes heavily, then finally*
and suddenly stands up.)
And now I will go. (*Beat.*) Before I drink too much. I do not
want to drink too much. John, will you see me to a cab?
(RYDER *stands and takes his arm.* MACREADY *turns to the others*
and points.)
A good day! A very good day it has been! Do not be
disheartened!
WEMYSS: (*Standing*) Actually we can help. We're leaving as well.
Let's go, Catherine.
MISS WEMYSS: (*To the others*) Thank you for letting me join you.
I have enjoyed myself very much.
(WEMYSS *takes* MACREADY'*s arm from* RYDER *and helps him*
out. CATHERINE *follows.* RYDER *watches them go.*)
CLARK: Why should we be disheartened? He said he thought
rehearsals were going well. I think rehearsals are going well.

7

MRS POPE: Please sit and stay, Mr Ryder. Unless you have to . . . (*Beat.*)

RYDER: No. (*He looks around the table.*) I don't have to . . . Thank you. I'd like to very much.
(*He sits back down. Pause.*)
Any idea who Mr Forrest will get to play Macduff?

TILTON: (*Before anyone can answer*) Ever seen Macready act?

MRS POPE: We're rehearsing with – .

TILTON: I mean from the audience. I have seen him many many times. (*Beat.*) Each time – it gets even worse.

MRS POPE: (*To* RYDER) Sorry, he's – .

RYDER: (*Holding up his hand*) No, no, please, don't – . Not for my sake. Just – .

CLARK: He's been fine to work with. (*Beat.*) I've worked with worse.

MRS POPE: He actually spent some time with me on a scene he isn't even in.

BRIDGES: I saw his Richard in Philadelphia on his last tour.
(*Beat.*) I don't much like that sort of acting. It's not why I go to the theatre.

CLARK: People like it.

TILTON: English people like it.

BRADSHAW: Not just English people. He's performed all around the – .

TILTON: Then people who want to be English people. They like it.

BRADSHAW: Maybe.

BRIDGES: Rich people like it.

TILTON: I agree with that too.

MRS POPE: The Astor Place Opera House people will like it. So he'll do fine. We'll do fine.

BRIDGES: As long as there's an audience.

TILTON: I wouldn't want such an audience.

MRS POPE: I say take what you can get.
(*Short pause.*)

BRIDGES: On my own, I never go to the Astor Place.

MRS POPE: It's expensive.

BRADSHAW: The dressing-rooms are rather nice though.

8

MRS POPE: They are, aren't they?
(*Short pause.*)
RYDER: I've – . (*Beat.*) I have played Macduff.
BRADSHAW: English actors I'll wager are very different from
    American actors.
MRS POPE: I hear when they go out – like this, as a group – they
    only speak in verse to each other.
RYDER: (*Quickly*) No, that's not true. We don't.
(*Others laugh.*)
We really don't. (*He realizes the joke and laughs with the others.*)
TILTON: I've worked with English actors. The first thing you learn
    is never leave out your money.
MRS POPE: When someone's passing through – when anyone is –
    and you know you can't find him again, you do not leave out
    your money. It has nothing to do with being – .
BRIDGES: Are you enjoying America, Mr Ryder?
CLARK: You've been before?
RYDER: No, I haven't. (*Beat.*) That's why Mr Macready, well,
    besides wanting the company, he thought I should see for
    myself. He said, John, you are not going to believe this. I want
    to be there to see your face.
(*Beat.*)
(THOMAS FISHER, JANE BASS, HELEN BURTON, *and* ANNE
HOLLAND – *all actors working with* EDWIN FORREST *at the
Broadway Theatre – enter, on their way to* TILTON'*s table which
he has been saving for them.*)
FISHER: (*While entering*) This one? Is this our table? How many – ?
(*Starts to count chairs.*)
MISS BASS: (*To* MRS POPE *at a distance*) Hello. How are you?
(MRS POPE *smiles and nods.*)
FISHER: We'll need another chair.
TILTON: Who's – ?
FISHER: Ned and Robert are at the bar getting the drinks.
CLARK: You can use these chairs.
FISHER: (*Goes to the table for the chairs*) Nice to see you.
CLARK: And you. (*Beat.*) You know – .
FISHER: Of course I do. Why don't you – . If you want.
MRS POPE: We're leaving. I'm leaving. We've been here how long?

9

FISHER: (*Taking the chair back to the other tables*) Another time then.

BRADSHAW: Absolutely.

(*The* MACREADY *table now watches the other table.*)

TILTON: (*To* MISS BASS) How's Scott? Anyone seen Scott?

MISS BASS: Ned spoke to him. (*Beat.*) The doctor wants him to sleep.

MISS BURTON: He wanted to come out with us.

(*She smiles and shakes her head.*)

MISS HOLLAND: He's going to be fine.

TILTON: Someone was saying they'd seen him drinking.

MISS BASS: Tonight?

TILTON: They said this tonight, yes.

FISHER: He didn't seem himself, did he? Even in the dressing-room. (*Beat.*) And he never dries.

MISS HOLLAND: He dried tonight?

FISHER: I think so. (*Beat.*) I'm not sure, but I think so. Sometimes with Scott it's hard to tell.

MISS HOLLAND: (*To* MISS BURTON) Save a place for Robert.

(MISS BURTON *looks at her and moves over a chair.*)

(EDWIN FORREST *and* ROBERT JONES, *also an actor with Forrest's Broadway Theatre company, enter carrying the drinks.*)

FORREST: (*While entering*) I'm spilling. (*To* JONES, *who is behind him*) Watch your step, don't slip. (*Beat.*) Someone should get a cloth and – . I don't want anyone to slip.

MISS BASS: (*Getting up*) I'll ask at the bar.

CLARK: We have a cloth. (*To* BRIDGES) Give me that. Give me the cloth.

(BRIDGES *does.*)

(*Holding up the cloth*) We have one.

FORREST: Thank you.

MISS BASS: I'll take it.

(*She takes the cloth.* FORREST *looks at* JONES.)

JONES: Clark. Charlie Clark.

FORREST: Thank you, Mr Clark. (*He starts to turn, stops, looks back at* CLARK.) Have we worked together?

CLARK: No. No, sir. (*Beat.*) Not yet. (*Laughs.*) Hopefully some day.

(FORREST *nods*.)

JONES: Charlie is – . In fact, you all are, aren't you? Working with Mr Macready on his *Macbeth*.

MRS POPE: We are. That's right.

FORREST: And it's going well?

(*They nod*.)

Good.

(*He winks at them and goes to the other table*.)

JONES: (*To the Macready table*) If you'd like to join – .

RYDER: I'd love to. Thanks.

(*He gets up*.)

(*Introducing himself*) Ryder. John Ryder.

JONES: How do you do? English?

RYDER: That's right.

CLARK: (*To others*) Why don't we . . . He's asked us. I'm going to.

(*He gets up*.)

MRS POPE: (*Getting up*) I can just stay a minute more.

BRADSHAW: Me too. One minute.

(*They move towards the other table, carrying their drinks.*

FORREST *is at the table beginning to serve*.)

FORREST: Who doesn't have a glass? Who wants wine? Who wants beer? (*Beat*.) Why don't I just pass it around.

RYDER: I heard you had a problem during the performance tonight.

(*Short pause*.)

FORREST: We did, yes. (*Beat*.) Poor Mr Scott, he – .

TILTON: I told them, Ned.

FORREST: (*Turns to* TILTON, *then back to* RYDER) Then you know. (*To others*) Please, help yourselves. (*Beat*.)

(*To* RYDER) Have *we* worked together?

RYDER: I've never performed in America. Not that I have anything against it. (*Beat*.) I'm a friend of Mr Macready's. I help him.

FORREST: I've been to England.

RYDER: Of course I know that. I've seen you – .

FORREST: Perhaps I saw you do something there.

RYDER: Perhaps.

FORREST: I'm sure I have. (*Stares at* RYDER *then turns to* FISHER.)

Mr Fisher, I've a few notes about tonight that I'd like to give
before I forget them. That's if you have a moment.

FISHER: Of course, Ned.

FORREST: Bring your chair.

(FISHER *brings his chair and sits next to* FORREST. *Others have
sat as well, except for* RYDER.)

RYDER: (*A little too loud*) What role was the poor man who hurt
himself playing?

(*Short pause. Others choose to consciously ignore Ryder's
question.*)

FORREST: (*Barely audible, to* FISHER) First let me say, what I
thought you were doing in our first scene was quite
laudable . . .

TILTON: (*To others*) You just missed Macready himself.

BRIDGES: He was with us. He bought us . . .

(*Conversations begin. Small groups of two or three, with only*
RYDER *excluded.*)

CLARK: I've got work in Cincinnati whenever I want it.

MISS BURTON: They all say that. Then you get to Cincinnati.

CLARK: Not this time. I believe these people. (*Beat.*) These people
are different.

MISS BURTON: Go to Cincinnati then.

(*Many overlapping conversations now so no one is
understandable. This goes on for a few moments and then:
blackout.*)

SCENE 2

Projection: 1 a.m.

Parlour, Edwin Forrest's house. A few chairs, a bookcase, etc.
    FORREST *and* MISS BASS *sit in chairs, fairly near to each other and
occasionally glance at each other. They also have glasses in their hands.*
BRADSHAW *stands at the bookcase browsing through the books.* RYDER
stands looking through a scrapbook. Long pause. RYDER *closes the
scrapbook, sets it on a table, notices a silver snuffbox and picks it up.*

RYDER: This is beautiful.

FORREST: (*Turns to* RYDER) Read what it says. (*Beat.*) Read it out loud so Mr Bradshaw can hear.

(BRADSHAW *stops browsing.*)

RYDER: (*Reading from the snuffbox*) 'Presented to Edwin Forrest, Esq., by the members of the Sheffield Theatrical Company, as a mark of their esteem for him as an ACTOR and a MAN.' (*Beat.*)

FORREST: Something to cherish.

RYDER: Certainly . . .

FORREST: Coming as it does from actors.

(*Short pause.*)

BRADSHAW: This was when you were in England . . .

FORREST: The last time. Let me see it. I haven't noticed it for a long time.

(RYDER *hands him the box.* MISS BASS *gets up and goes to* FORREST *to look at the box. Short pause.*)

(*To* MISS BASS) They had a nice little ceremony. The man who made the speech was a very lousy actor.

(*He smiles, others laugh lightly.*)

Brooke, I think his name was. Do you know him, Mr Ryder?

RYDER: I don't know. I – . I don't think so.

FORREST: I thought being English . . .

RYDER: Maybe I do. I don't know. (*Beat.*) Brooke? I don't know.

(FORREST *hands* RYDER *back the box.*)

It is a beautiful box.

(RYDER *goes and puts it back on the table.*)

FORREST: (*Holds up a decanter*) Would anyone – ?

RYDER: I'm fine, thank you.

(FORREST *turns to* BRADSHAW, *who shakes his head and goes back to browsing. He turns to* MISS BASS, *who now sits on the arm of his chair.*)

MISS BASS: (*Holding up her glass*) I haven't touched what I have.

(FORREST *puts the decanter down without pouring a drink.*)

FORREST: (*Without looking at* RYDER) Have you already gone through both scrapbooks, Mr Ryder?

RYDER: I – . Both? No. I didn't know there were two. I've only seen this – .

13

FORREST: Miss Bass knows where the other one is kept.

MISS BASS: I'll get it.

(*She goes to a table, opens a drawer, takes out a book.*)

FORREST: I call that section the Shakespeare Corner, Mr Bradshaw.

BRADSHAW: I can see why.

(*Laughs.*)

FORREST: Warburton's edition is certainly worth a look.

BRADSHAW: Which is . . . ?

FORREST: To your left. (*Beat.*) Up one. Two over. There. That's right.

(BRADSHAW *takes out a book.*)

I have nearly all the editions of Shakespeare's work. Even – . (*Stops himself. Smiles.*) But we'll get to that. (*Turns to* MISS BASS, *who has the scrapbook.*) I'll take that, please. (*Turns back to* BRADSHAW.) The actor's work – I don't have to tell you – is much more than what is on the stage. These are but some necessary tools for one's investigations. (*Takes the scrapbook and opens it.*) Come here, Mr Ryder. I plan to exhaust all of your enthusiasm as well as your patience.

RYDER: I'm the one who asked to see – .

FORREST: (*Pointing out things in the scrapbook*) Here I am as Richard III. (*Smiles.*) This was in Dublin, you'll be interested to know.

(FORREST *stares at the picture. Pause.* RYDER *looks to* MISS BASS *and then to* BRADSHAW *who has come to look over* FORREST's *shoulder. Finally, he turns the page.*)

Romeo.

(FORREST *stares at the picture, then sniffles, takes out a handkerchief and wipes a tearing eye.* RYDER *watches this, aware that he has no idea what is going on and uncomfortable because of this.*)

I also played Mercutio. First I played Mercutio. I was only a boy then.

(*Smiles at* MISS BASS, *who smiles and takes his hand.*)

Mr Wallack was the Romeo. He was much too old. Much. He should have known better. (*Beat.*) Someone should have told him. Been honest with him. (*Sighs and stands.*) I

14

promised to show you something, didn't I, Mr Bradshaw.
Excuse me. (*He goes off.*)

BRADSHAW: (*To* RYDER) What's he . . . ?

(RYDER *shrugs.*)

I think I will have a little of that.

(*Pours himself a drink. Atmosphere in the room has suddenly relaxed.*)

RYDER: (*To* MISS BASS) Have you worked with Mr Forrest before? (*Beat.*) I mean before this season.

(*She looks at* BRADSHAW, *then back at* RYDER.)

MISS BASS: Yes. Yes I have.

RYDER: Then maybe you can help me: Do you think he was being serious when he said he wanted me for Macduff?

MISS BASS: Yes, I'm sure he was being serious, Mr Ryder. (*Beat.*) He needs a – .

RYDER: Sometimes you don't know. People say all sorts of things. (*Beat.*) Especially late at night.

MISS BASS: Rehearsals are tomorrow. I'm sure he expects you there.

BRADSHAW: You know the part.

RYDER: In England I've played it a hundred – .

(*He stops himself as* MRS CATHERINE FORREST *enters: she is in her dressing-gown. Awkward pause.*)

MRS FORREST: I thought I heard voices. (*Beat.*) Is my husband here or do you just come on your own now, Miss Bass?

BRADSHAW: He went to get something.

(MRS FORREST *begins to go off in that direction.*)

MISS BASS: How are you, Mrs Forrest?

(*She ignores this and goes off. Beat.*)

RYDER: I hadn't realized he had a wife.

(*From off: the sound of an argument,* FORREST *and his wife shouting at each other; though exactly what they are shouting about cannot be heard.* RYDER, BRADSHAW, *and* MISS BASS *try to ignore what they hear is happening.* RYDER *pours himself a drink.*)

BRADSHAW: (*To* RYDER) Have you seen the – .

(*He nods towards the bookcase.*)

RYDER: I haven't had the chance yet. But I'd love too.

(*He goes to the bookcase.*)

15

BRADSHAW: An extraordinary collection.

(*They pretend to browse, as the argument continues off. Finally* FORREST *enters alone, carrying a large book.*)

FORREST: (*While entering*) Pope's edition is also worth looking through. But before that . . . (*Beat. Holds up book.*) Here is what I wanted to show you. (*He sits.*) The most precious thing I own.

(RYDER *and* BRADSHAW *come closer.*)

I dare say, I believe it to be the only First Folio in the New World.

RYDER: First Folio – ?

(*He instinctively reaches for it.*)

FORREST: Gentle. Gentle, Mr Ryder. (*Beat.*) She breathes. This book. She lives.

(*He opens it and reads.*)

'Mr William Shakespeare's Comedies, Histories & Tragedies. Published according to the True original copies. London. Printed by Issac Jaggard and Ed. Blout, 1623.'

(*Pause.* FORREST *has heard something.*)

Now she's crying.

(MRS FORREST *can be heard crying in the next room.*)

(*To* RYDER) Feel the cover.

(*He does.*)

As smooth as a child's face. As smooth as a face. (*He rubs his hand across* MISS BASS'*s face.*) What one needs to study to be a Shakespearean actor. (*Gently pats the book.*) The truth lies in our hands. (*Beat.*) The ignorance of the world knows no bounds, Mr Ryder. I have twice been criticized for reading 'dead vast' instead of saying 'dead waste'. Some quartos have it even as 'wast' – whatever that is supposed to mean – and also as 'waist' – W–A–I–S–T. (*Laughs.*) But in here, Mr Ryder, our true authority, it is 'vast'. (*Beat.*) 'Vast' for the vacancy and void of night. For the deserted emptiness. Not 'waste'. Not for what has been thrown away. 'Vast'! For the hole, the H–O–L–E! The loss of what is, what was, a loss that shall always remain a loss! (*Beat.*) You study. You learn. (*Beat.*) Like a face. That smooth. Rub your face against the book and feel it. Against your flesh.

16

(RYDER *takes the book and rubs it against his face, then hands it to* BRADSHAW, *who does the same. Pause.*)
(*Without looking at* RYDER.) Some of Macduff's lines we cut, Mr Ryder. I shall give you such cuts tomorrow.
(*Pause.*)
Poor Scott, cut his finger off from here. (*Holds up his finger.*) Blood was everywhere. Somehow it even got on the sheets. (*Beat.*) Big stain on Desdemona's sheets. I noticed this as I – . I was holding the pillow. (*He looks up at them.*) Sometimes you lose yourself so much in a role. (*Beat.*) Sometimes you – . (*Beat.*) Sometimes you are so lost.
(MRS FORREST'*s crying is louder for a moment.*)
RYDER: Maybe we better . . . (*Beat.*) If I'm going to be ready for rehearsal.
(*He tries to smile.*)
FORREST: I was good as Othello tonight. They got their money's worth.
(*Short pause.* RYDER *doesn't know whether to leave or not. Blackout.*)

SCENE 3

Projection: 2 a.m.

Parlour of Macready's rooms at the New York Hotel.
   MISS WEMYSS *sits alone.* RYDER *has just entered.*

RYDER: I'm sorry, I – . Is Mr Macready . . .?
MISS WEMYSS: He'll be right out. He's just in there.
   (RYDER *nods. Pause. He paces, not knowing whether to stay or go; she watches him, smiling when she catches his eye.*)
RYDER: He left me a note. (*Beat.*) Downstairs. When I came in they gave me the note. (*Beat.*) It said he wanted to see me as soon as I . . . (*Beat.*) I just got in. It's probably too late.
MISS WEMYSS: I don't know.
   (*Short pause.*)
RYDER: (*Putting on his hat*) Tell him I – .
   (MACREADY *enters in his dressing-gown.*)

17

MACREADY: Come in, John, please come in.

RYDER: It's very late.

MACREADY: Thank you for coming. Sit down. I'll fix us a drink.

RYDER: I've had plenty tonight.

MACREADY: A nightcap never hurts.

(*Pause. He pours their drinks.*)

You've met Miss Wemyss?

RYDER: Tonight. At the tavern. With her father – .

MACREADY: Of course you have! Of course! Where is my head?

(*Laughs to himself.*)

(*To* MISS WEMYSS) And what about you, my dear, what may I get you?

MISS WEMYSS: I don't wish anything, Mr Macready. I am content as I am.

(*He suddenly bursts out laughing.*)

MACREADY: I don't know what it is about her, John, but everything she says makes me laugh.

(MISS WEMYSS *smiles at* RYDER.)

RYDER: I think we should talk in the morning.

(WEMYSS *enters carrying a teapot.*)

WEMYSS: (*While entering*) This is all I could – . From the kitchen. They insisted they put it in a teapot though. I don't understand this thinking. (*Beat.*) I had to stand down there and watch them pour a whole bottle into a teapot.

(*Shakes his head.*)

MACREADY: (*Holding up the decanter*) Now pour it into here, Mr Wemyss. (*Turns to* RYDER.) We were beginning to get a little low.

(WEMYSS *pours the liquor out of the pot and into the bottle. He is a bit drunk.*)

Your daughter just said something very funny. Very funny.

(WEMYSS *turns to his daughter and smiles and continues to pour.*)

(*To* RYDER) What did she say?

RYDER: I don't know. Why is Mr Wemyss – ? What's he doing here?

MACREADY: (*To* MISS WEMYSS) What is it you said?

MISS WEMYSS: I don't remember any more.

(MACREADY *bursts out laughing, then turns to* RYDER, *patting*

18

WEMYSS *on the shoulder*.)

MACREADY: Frederick here wanted a little advice, didn't you?

WEMYSS: You've been very helpful, William.

MACREADY: His daughter – . This is his daughter. She wishes to become an actress. Isn't this true, my dear?
(*She smiles*.)

WEMYSS: She has the looks for it, I think. Look at her.
(*She smiles again at* RYDER.)

MACREADY: And – . (*Beat*.) You – . What? You wondered, correct? If there might be some place in London – . To learn. He thinks she should learn in London. That says something does it not? (*Beat*.) Someone to learn from.

WEMYSS: Someone to even befriend . . .
(*Turns to his daughter*.) You don't know what can happen when a young woman is that far away from her family. (*Turns to* MACREADY.) She has a lovely family. Five daughters. They take care of each other.

MACREADY: (*To* RYDER) I am going to look into matters for her. I shall see what there might be for – . I don't know. (*Beat*.) Perhaps an apprenticeship? (*Beat*.) Perhaps at Drury Lane? How would that strike you, my dear?
(*He smiles*.)

WEMYSS: Drury Lane would be excellent.

MACREADY: I cannot promise of course.

WEMYSS: No one is asking for a promise, William. No one. Are we?

MISS WEMYSS: I'm not.
(MACREADY *looks at her, smiles and finally sighs a drunk sigh. Pause.*)

RYDER: What did you want to see me about?

MACREADY: Drink, John. We have a whole new teapot full of drink. (*Gestures for* RYDER *to take his drink*. RYDER *doesn't move*.) Oh yes. That. (*Turns to* MISS WEMYSS.) What would you do, Miss Wemyss? Would you ignore the threats?

RYDER: What threats? What are you talking about?
(MACREADY *laughs and nods at* RYDER.)

MACREADY: (*To* MISS WEMYSS) Now everyone is getting worried. Don't panic, Mr Ryder, please.

(*Laughs. Pause. He stops laughing and turns to* RYDER.)
Mr Wemyss has been telling me that we are under threat. Or
do I exaggerate?

WEMYSS: No. (*Beat.*) Mr Macready's life is, I believe, in some
danger.

RYDER: For what? Who – ?

WEMYSS: There have been letters. I have one here. (*Takes out a
letter, hands it to* RYDER.) I didn't want to mention it at the
tavern, with – .
(RYDER *starts to hand the letter to* MACREADY.)

MACREADY: I've seen it, John. You read it. See what you think.

WEMYSS: Though most in the company have been – . *Are* aware at
least that something . . . You feel it in the air, I suppose. And
we've all heard I guess that there are persons who are
upset – .

RYDER: For what reason?!

MACREADY: Because I dare to perform the noble Thane on the
same night in the same city as does the sainted American, Mr
Edwin Forrest! (*Turns to* WEMYSS.) Is that not the true
reason?

WEMYSS: I don't know. (*Beat.*) Maybe. I know it's what you
think.

MACREADY: Of course it's the reason for these attacks! A
perceived competition with their idol, their native idol!
(*Beat.*) Ridiculous. (*Beat.*) Sheer effrontery – on my part.
This is how they see it. Pure gall. And of course it would be
upsetting. On the same night! For all to compare! Of course
they are worried! (*Laughs.*) And an Englishman, no less!
Look at the spelling. The illiterate bastards. Probably Irish.

RYDER: I don't understand what they're demanding.

MACREADY: Short of a complete surrender and my going home
immediately, you mean. (*Laughs to himself.*) All in good
time. All in good time. (*Beat.*)

WEMYSS: The letters are meant to frighten – .

RYDER: (*To* MACREADY) And you take the threats seriously?

MACREADY: I don't. (*Laughs.*) I don't. But others may. (*Beat.*) So
I am suggesting that we contact Mr Forrest, present him
with this irksome situation we, as guests, now confront in his

20

homeland, and no doubt he shall do the honourable thing and see fit to perform some other of his multitude of roles that evening. (*Beat.*) Let's say *Metamora*. (*Beat.*) I understand he is especially convincing as an Indian. Americans can be, you know. An Englishman would be hopeless as a savage. A pity I will not be able to see this performance myself. (*Beat.*) John, I think I am asking you to do this.

RYDER: I doubt if Mr Forrest will change his repertoire at this late – .

MACREADY: He has to!

(*Short pause.*)

He has many plays – they are cast – they can be mounted. I have scheduled only *Macbeth*. I have only a company for *Macbeth*. It would be impossible for me to do anything else. (*Beat.*) Besides, I understand after the accident tonight he doesn't even have a Macduff. So if he needs to explain to the public – .

RYDER: He has a new Macduff.

(*Pause.*)

He asked me. (*Beat.*) You have Clark. You wanted Clark. I didn't have anything to do. I know I'm here to help you, but I can do both. I know the role for Christ's sake! (*Beat.*) I told Forrest I would have to speak with you first. And if you objected . . . (*Beat.*) He was desperate. But . . . Do you object?

MACREADY: (*Without looking at him*) We are a fraternity, John – the acting fraternity. We know no borders. Have no flags. (*Beat.*) So how can I object to helping out Mr Forrest. Wouldn't he do the same for me? I'll get someone else to speak with him. Someone with less to lose.

RYDER: That's not fair.

WEMYSS: I'd be happy to.

RYDER: Forrest's performance is sold out. It would be nearly impossible at this point to change the schedule.

MACREADY: (*Suddenly turns on him*) Men and women are being threatened with violence, John, and you talk about an inconvenience?!! (*Beat.*) I do not say this for myself. Do you understand? (*Beat.*) But these actors work under my protection. I have their safety as my responsibility. (*Sips his drink.*) We have not yet sold out. (*Beat.*) Two *Macbeth*s in one evening may be too much for New York to bear. (*Beat.*) I cannot change. I have told you why. If he does not, these scoundrels, these ignorant hooligans have the guts, I'm afraid, to attempt what they have threatened. Does Mr Forrest realize what he will be instigating? Consciously or not. Will he alone accept the responsibility for our well-being?

(*Short pause.*)

I'm sure we'll be fine. (*Shrugs.*) I'm pleased you found work. I truly am.

RYDER: He asked me. I didn't seek it. I must have said no ten times.

(*Laughs.*)

MACREADY: So – what else could you do? (*Reaches for the letter, takes it from* RYDER, *and begins to look at it again.*) I knew nothing of any problems. Any such – tensions. Where did they come from? I should have been warned. To hate one simply because one is accomplished. (*Beat.*) Had I known . . .

(*Shakes his head.*)

RYDER: You knew – I knew that there's some resentment when any English actor – .

MACREADY: I am not any English actor! (*Beat.*) And I knew of no such resentment, John!! (*Sits and sighs.*) Such incidents make one long for home even more.

(MISS WEMYSS *starts to stand.*)

Please everyone, there is no need to hurry off.

(*She sits. Short pause.*)

RYDER: It's very late.

MACREADY: Yes it is. Yes.

(*Pause.*)

I wrote Mrs Macready. (*To* RYDER) This was where I was when you came in. (*To* MISS WEMYSS) You didn't mind, did you? Being left on your own?

(*Short pause.*)

I spoke of this loneliness. Being away from home. (*Beat.*)
She must be getting tired of such letters. (*Laughs to himself.*)
But it is like being suspended upon the edge of a cliff. This is
how much of your country feels to me, Mr Wemyss. As a
cliff. (WEMYSS *nods*) I try to go to sleep and a hundred devils
attack me. (*Beat.*) And tie me up. (*Beat.*) Little devils.
(*Yawns.*) If I did not know how important what I bring is.
(*Beat.*) The need. When one is hearing Shakespeare spoken
correctly for the first time. (*Smiles.*) It is an honour. And it is
a burden. One I shall gladly pass on to younger men. (*Beat.*)
When they emerge. (*Beat.*) I'm tired. Don't go yet.
(*Pause.*)

WEMYSS: I have been to Drury Lane myself once. This was years
ago when I was a much younger man. (*Beat.*) I think my
daughter could be very comfortable there. I have told all my
children – there is nothing like England. Nothing in the
world.

MISS WEMYSS: Mr Macready has not offered to . . .
(*Beat.*)

MACREADY: (*Looks at her and smiles*) I shall. I do. (*Beat.*) But will
I remember I've offered in the morning? (*Laughs.*) Let me
think about it.
(*Pause.* MACREADY *sits, staring at nothing.* MISS WEMYSS
smiles. WEMYSS *stands behind Macready's chair and sips his
drink.* RYDER *doesn't know whether to leave or not.*
Blackout.)

SCENE 4

Projection: The next day, the afternoon.

*A bare stage, which represents the stages of the Astor Place Opera
House and the Broadway Theatre, during rehearsals of the two*
Macbeths.

a) *Broadway Theatre*
Drums. Then thunder. The THREE WITCHES (Misses Bass, Burton
and Holland) *are on.* (Act I. iii)

23

1ST WITCH: . . . nine times nine,
    Shall he dwindle, peak, and pine.
    Though his bark cannot be lost.
    Yet it shall be tempest-tost.
2ND WITCH: Show me, show me.
3RD WITCH: Here I have a pilot's thumb,
    Wracked as homeward he did come.
    (*Drum within.*)
ALL: A drum! a drum!
    Macbeth doth come.
    (MACBETH [Forrest] *and* BANQUO [Jones] *enter.*)
MACBETH: So foul and fair a day I have not seen.
BANQUO: How far is't called to Forres? What are these,
    That look not like the inhabitants o' th' earth,
    And yet are on't?
MACBETH: Speak, if you can. What are you?
1ST WITCH: All hail, Macbeth! Hail to thee, Thane of Glamis!
2ND WITCH: All hail, Macbeth! Hail to thee, Thane of Cawdor!
3RD WITCH: All hail, Macbeth, that shalt be King hereafter!
BANQUO: Good sir, why do you start, and seem to fear
    Things that do sound so fair? To me you speak not,
    Speak then to me, who neither beg nor fear
    Your favours nor your hate.
1ST WITCH: Hail!
2ND WITCH: Hail!
3RD WITCH: Hail!
1ST WITCH: Lesser than Macbeth, and greater.
2ND WITCH: Not so happy, yet much happier.
3RD WITCH: Thou shalt get kings, though thou be none.
    So all hail, Macbeth and Banquo!
MACBETH: Stay, you imperfect speakers, say from whence
    You owe this strange intelligence, or why
    Upon this blasted heath you stop our way
    With such prophetic greeting. Speak, I charge you.
    (WITCHES *run off,* MACBETH *and* BANQUO *give chase.*)

b) *Astor Place Opera House*
The THREE WITCHES (*all male*: Bridges *and two older men*, John Sefton *and* Chippindale), MACBETH (Macready) *and* BANQUO (Bradshaw).

1ST WITCH: Hail!
2ND WITCH: Hail!
3RD WITCH: Hail!
1ST WITCH: Lesser than Macbeth, and greater.
2ND WITCH: Not so happy, yet much happier.
3RD WITCH: Thou shalt get kings, though thou be none.
    So all hail, Macbeth and Banquo!
MACBETH: By Sinell's death I know I am Thane of Glamis,
    But how of Cawdor? The Thane of Cawdor lives,
    A prosperous gentleman; and to be King
    Stands not within the prospect of belief.
    No more than to be Cawdor. Say from whence
    You owe this strange intelligence.
    (WITCHES *run off*, MACBETH *and* BANQUO *give chase*.)

c) *Broadway Theatre*
The KING (Mr Blakeley) *and* LADY MACBETH (Mrs Fanny Wallack). *Fanfare*. (Act I. vi)

KING: Where's the Thane of Cawdor?
    We coursed him at the heels and had a purpose
    To be his purveyor; but he rides well,
    And his great love, sharp as his spur, hath holp him
    To his home before us. Fair and noble hostess,
    Give me your hand.
    (*They go off. Fanfare. People run across the stage with torches.*
    Then out of the shadows enters MACBETH [Forrest].) (Act I.
    vii)
MACBETH: If it were done when 'tis done, then 'twere well
    It were done quickly. If th' assassination
    Could trammel up the consequence, and catch
    With his surcease success, that but this blow
    Might be the be-all and the end-all; here,
    But here upon this bank and shoal of time,

We'ld jump the life to come. But in these cases
We still have judgement here, that we but teach
Bloody instructions, which, being taught, return
To plague th' inventor. This even-handed justice
Commends . . .

d) *Astor Place Opera House*
MACBETH (Macready) *alone*. (Act I. vii)

MACBETH: Will plead like angels, trumpet-tongued against
The deep damnation of his taking-off;
And pity, like a naked new-born babe
Striding the blast, or heaven's cherubim horsed
Upon the sightless couriers of the air,
Shall blow the horrid deed in every eye
That tears shall drown the wind. I have no spur
To prick the sides of my intent, but only
Vaulting ambition, which o'erleaps itself
And falls on th' other –
(*Pause. Finally* MACBETH [Macready] *turns towards the wings
and gives a small nod, and* LADY MACBETH [Mrs Pope] *enters.*)
How now? What news?
MACREADY: (*To* MRS POPE) Closer. Closer. There. Now look at
me. (*Beat.*) I look at them and you look at me. Thank you.
(*Beat.*)
MACBETH: How now? What news?

e) *Broadway Theatre*
BANQUO (Jones) *enters.* (Act II. i)

BANQUO: Who's there?
(MACBETH [Forrest] *enters with a torch.*)
MACBETH: A friend. Get thee to bed.
(BANQUO *exits.*)
Is this a dagger which I see before me,
The handle toward my hand? Come, let me clutch thee!
I have thee not, and yet I see thee still.
Art thou not, fatal vision, sensible
To feeling as to sight? or art thou but

A dagger of the mind, a false creation,
Proceeding from the heat-oppressed brain?
I see thee yet, in form as palpable
As this which now I draw.
Thou marshall'st me the way . . .

f) *Both theatres are represented.*
BOTH MACBETHS (Macready *and* Forrest) *now continue the speech together, though not necessarily in sync.*

BOTH MACBETHS: . . . that I was going,
        Mine eyes are made the fools o' th' other senses,
        Or else worth all the rest. I see thee still,
        And on thy blade and dudgeon gouts of blood,
        Which was not so before. There's no such thing.
        It is a bloody business which informs
        This to mine eyes.
        (*Lights begin to fade on* FORREST.)
                        Now o'er the one half-world
        Nature seems dead, and wicked dreams abuse
        The curtained sleep.
        (MACREADY *is alone now. The stage represents only the Astor Place Opera House.*)
MACBETH: Thou sure and firm-set earth,
        Hear not my steps which way they walk, for fear
        The very stones prate on my whereabout
        And take the present horror from the time,
        Which suits with it. Whiles I threat, he lives;
        Words to the heat of deeds too cold breath gives.

g) *Broadway Theatre*
Very loud pounding or knocking is suddenly heard. PORTER (Tilton) *hurries on.* (Act II. iii)

PORTER: Here's a knocking indeed! If a man were porter of hell
        gate, he should have old turning the key. (*Another knock.*)
        Knock, knock, knock. Who's there, in th' other devil's
        name?
        (*Beat.*)

27

TILTON: Wait, I think I jumped. It's what? Is it 'knock, knock'? Or 'knock, knock, knock'? Which is the first, the two or the three knocks? (*Beat.*) Please, which is the first?!

PROMPTER: (*Off*) It's the three 'knocks' first.

TILTON: Really? (*Beat.*) Thank you. (*Beat.*) Sorry. (*Goes back to his position, then suddenly breaks it.*) Now let me get this straight. It's the three 'knocks', then the two 'knocks', right? And then it's the three again, am I correct? And then it's the two again?

PROMPTER: That is correct.

TILTON: So it's three 'knocks' and the devil's name line. Then two 'knocks' and the Belzebub.

PROMPTER: (*Off*) The three 'knocks' are with the Belzebub and the two are with the devil's name.

TILTON: What?

PROMPTER: (*Off*) And it's the devil's name line that comes first. (*Beat.*) After the *three* 'knocks'.
(TILTON *stares in disbelief.*)
Then the third one – also after three 'knocks' – is the English tailor bit. Then comes 'too cold for hell'. (*Beat.*) After three more 'knocks'. (*Beat.*) I'm sorry, after *two* more 'knocks'. (*Beat.*) Yes, that's right, it is two more 'knocks' for the last one. Is that clear?
(*Short pause.* TILTON *tries to shake off confusion.*)

TILTON: (*Rubs his eyes*) Let me start again. (*As he exits*) I'm sorry to hold everyone up.
(*He leaves. Pounding. He hurries on.*)

PORTER: Here's a knocking indeed!
(*Stops himself.*)

TILTON: I don't have the faintest idea what I'm saying now. All I'm thinking about is how many goddamn 'knocks' I have!
(*Short pause.* FORREST *enters with others in the company.*)
Sorry, Ned.

FORREST: Take your time.

TILTON: I'm fine. I knew it. Ask anyone and they'll tell you I knew it perfect. (*Beat.*) I was just a little uncertain of the 'knocks'.
(*Awkward pause.*)

Would you mind if I . . . Just for now, if I said say as many
'knocks' as I want. As come out. That's what's . . .
FORREST: Say what you want. I mean it. (*To others*) Ready? Let's
continue.
(*He leaves with the others.*)
TILTON: (*As he exits, to the* PROMPTER, *off*) Hear that? I can say
as many 'knocks' as I damn well want!
(*He exits.*)

h) *Astor Place Opera House*
MRS POPE (Lady Macbeth) *stands to one side as* MACREADY
(Macbeth) *plays both* Macbeth *and* Lady Macbeth *in* Act II. ii.

MACREADY: (*As* Lady Macbeth) If he do bleed,
I'll gild the faces of the grooms withal,
For it must seem their guilt.
(*He runs off. Returns as* MACBETH *and knocks with his foot.*)
(*As* Macbeth)   Whence is that knocking?
How is't with me when every noise appals me?
What hands are here? Ha! they pluck out mine eyes.
Will all great Neptune's ocean wash this blood
Clean from my hand? No, this my hand will rather
The multitudinous seas incarnadine,
Making the green one red.
(*He hurries to a side and enters now as* LADY MACBETH.)
(*As* Lady Macbeth) My hands are of your colour, but I
shame
To wear a heart so white.
(*He knocks with his foot.*)
                    I hear knocking
At the south entry.
MACREADY: And blah-blah-blah. Whatever the lines. More
knocking. (*Knocks with his foot.*) Something about retiring to
the bedroom. I take you by the hand. Like this. Come here.
(MRS POPE *goes to him, he takes her hand.*)
MACBETH: To know my deed, 'twere best not know myself.
(*Knocks with his foot.*)
Wake Duncan with thy knocking! I would thou couldst.

MACREADY: Head on my shoulder. And look down. Down.
(*Beat. As they exit*) And I look out as we leave.
(*They exit.*)

i) *Broadway Theatre*
PORTER (Tilton) *alone on stage. Pause.*

TILTON: I've dried. I've never dried.
FORREST: (*Entering*) What's the line? Give him the line.
TILTON: I don't remember anything. What's my character?
What's the name of the play? (*Laughs.*) I'm kidding.
(*Laughs.*) I'm sorry everyone. My apologies to all of you. It's
one of those days.
(*Laughs.*)
FORREST: Just say your last line and we'll keep going.
(*He turns to go.*)
TILTON: What's my last line?
PROMPTER: (*Off*) 'I pray you remember the porter.'
(*Pause.* PORTER *alone on stage.*)
TILTON: Ready?
(*Sighs, then, unaware of the mistake he is making:*)
PORTER: I pray the porter remember.
(MACDUFF [Ryder] *enters.*)
MACDUFF: Was it so late, friend, ere you went to bed,
That you do lie so late?
TILTON: I don't know those lines. We cut those lines. I wasn't
supposed to know them.
FORREST: (*Entering*) You enter with me, Mr Ryder. Each from
different sides. (*Calls off*) What's the line?
PROMPTER: (*Off*) 'Our knocking has awaken.'
FORREST: Our knocking as awaken. (*Beat.*) From different sides.
RYDER: The rest is cut.
FORREST: I thought someone was giving Mr Ryder the cuts?!
(*They go.* TILTON *is alone.*)
TILTON: From my last line? (*Beat.*) What was my last line again?
PROMPTER: (*Off*) It's 'I pray you remember the porter.' It's not 'I
pray the porter remember.'
TILTON: 'I pray the . . .'

30

PROMPTER: Which is what you said the last time.
TILTON: I said – ? (*Beat.*) I couldn't have said . . . (*Beat.*) I did?
    I heard – .
FORREST: (*Off*) Please, Tilton, begin!
    (*Short pause.*)
TILTON: (*He does not know what to say*) I . . . Uh.

j) *Astor Place Opera House*
MACDUFF (Clark) *appears on a balcony.* (Act II. iii) MACBETH
(Macready) *is below.*

MACDUFF: Awake, awake!
    Ring the alarum bell! Murder and treason!
MACREADY: (*At the same time*) Faster! Faster!
    (*He bangs his hand on the floor to get* MACDUFF *to speak faster.*)
MACDUFF: Shake off this downy sleep, death's conterfeit,
    And look on death itself. Ring the bell.
    (*Bell rings. People hurry across the stage.* MACREADY *continues
    to get everyone to move faster.* LADY MACBETH [Mrs Pope]
    hurries on.*)
LADY MACBETH: What's the business,
    That such a hideous trumpet calls to parley
    The sleepers of the house?
MACREADY: Quicker!
    (LADY MACBETH *hurries out. Bell rings.* MACBETH *now slowly,
    very slowly, takes centre stage, listens to the bells ring, takes out
    the dagger from under his coat and, staring at the audience, drops
    it, then slowly exits.*)

k) *Broadway Theatre*
Thunder and lightning. MACBETH (Forrest) *and the* THREE
WITCHES (Misses Bass, Burton and Holland). (Act IV. i)
The WITCHES *sit on the ground.*

MACBETH: I conjure you, by that which you profess,
    Howe'er you come to know it, answer me.
1ST WITCH: Speak.
2ND WITCH: Demand.
3RD WITCH: We'll answer.

31

1ST WITCH: Say if th' hadst rather hear it from our mouths,
   Or from our masters.
MACBETH: Call 'em – .
   (*Stops himself. Goes to one of the* WITCHES *and pulls her dress up a little so a bit more of her attractive leg can be seen, then continues.*)
                        Call 'em. Let me see 'em.
ALL: Come, high or low,
   Thyself and office deftly show!
   (*Thunder and an explosion.*)

l) *Astor Place Opera House*
MACBETH (Macready), *the* THREE WITCHES (*the men*: Sefton, Bridges, Chippindale) *and* 1ST APPARITION. (Act IV. i)

1ST APPARITION: Macbeth, Macbeth, Macbeth, beware
      Macduff!
   Beware the Thane of Fife! Dismiss me. – Enough.
   (*Apparition leaves.*)
MACBETH: Whate'er thou art, for thy good caution, thanks:
   Thou hast harped my – .
   (*Stops himself. Goes to one of the* WITCHES *and pulls his dress down a little so less of his leg can be seen, then continues.*)
   Thou hast harp'd my fear aright.
1ST WITCH: Here's another,
   More potent than the first.
   (*Thunder and an explosion.*)

m) *Broadway Theatre*
MACDUFF (Ryder) *and* MALCOLM (Jones). (Act IV. iii)

MACDUFF: (*With great passion*)
            Fit to govern?
   No, not to live! O nation miserable,
   With an untitled tyrant bloody-sceptred,
   When shalt thou see thy wholesome days again,
   Since that the truest issue of thy throne
   By his own interdiction stands accursed,

And does blaspheme his breed? Oh my breast,
    Thy hope ends here!
    (*Beat. They begin to walk off.*)
JONES: Calm down, calm down. You've got the part.
    (*They exit.*)

o) *Astor Place Opera House*
Drums and colours. MALCOLM (Peter Arnold), SIWARD (Wemyss),
MACDUFF (Clark) *and* SOLDIERS *enter.* (Act V. vi)

MALCOLM: Now near enough. Your leavy screens throw down
    And show like those you are. You, worthy uncle,
    Shall with my cousin, your right noble son,
    Lead our first battle. Worthy Macduff and we
    Shall take upon's what else remains to do,
    According to our order.
SIWARD: Fare you well.
MACDUFF: Make all our trumpets speak, give them all breath,
    Those clamorous harbingers of blood and death.
    (*Alarms sound. They exit.*)
    (MACBETH [Macready] *enters.*) (Act V. vii)
MACBETH: They have tied me to a stake. I cannot fly,
    But bear-like I must fight the course. What's he
    That was not born of woman? Such a one
    Am I to fear, or none.
    (*Enter* YOUNG SIWARD [Bridges].)
YOUNG SIWARD: What is thy name?
MACBETH: Thou'lt be afraid to hear it.
    My name's Macbeth.
YOUNG SIWARD: The devil himself could not pronounce a title
    More hateful to mine ear.
    (*They fight. This should be a much stiffer battle than that which*
    FORREST *will fight.* YOUNG SIWARD *is slain.* MACBETH *drags
    him off.*)

p) *Broadway Theatre*
MACBETH (Forrest) *and* YOUNG SIWARD (Fisher) *enter fighting. This
should be quite a thrilling sword fight. Then* YOUNG SIWARD *is slain.*

33

MACBETH: Thou was born of woman.
    But swords I smile at, weapons laugh to scorn,
    Brandished by man that's of a woman born.
    (*He drags off the body.*)

q) *Astor Place Opera House*
Continuation of previous scene (Act v. vii). MACDUFF (Clark) *enters.*

MACDUFF: The way the noise is. Tyrant, show thy face!
    (MACBETH [Macready] *enters.*)
MACBETH: Why should I play the Roman fool and die
    On mine own sword? Whiles I see lives, the gashes
    Do better upon them.
MACDUFF: Turn, hellhound, turn!
MACBETH: Of all men else I have avoided thee.
    But get thee back! My soul is much charged
    With blood of thine already.
MACDUFF: I have no words;
    My voice is in my sword, thou bloodier villain
    Than terms can give thee out!
    (*They fight.*)
MACBETH: I bear a charmed life, which must not yield
    To one of woman born.
MACDUFF: Despair thy charm,
    And let the angel whom thou still hast served,
    Tell thee, Macduff was from his mother's womb
    Untimely ripped.
MACBETH: Accursed be that tongue that tells me so,
    For it hath cowed my better part of man!
MACDUFF: 'Here may you see the tyrant.'
MACBETH: Before my body
    I throw my warlike shield. Lay on, Macduff;
    And damned be him that first cries, 'Hold, enough!'
    (*They exit, fighting.*)
    (MALCOLM [Arnold], SIWARD [Wemyss], *and others enter.*)
    (Act v. ix)
MALCOLM: I would the friends we miss were safe arrived.
SIWARD: Some must go off; and yet, by these I see,

34

So great a day as this is cheaply bought.

MALCOLM: Macduff is missing, and your noble son.

(MACDUFF *enters with the bloody head of* MACBETH.)

SIWARD: And so, God be with him. Here comes newer comfort.

MACDUFF: Hail, King of Scotland!

ALL: Hail, King of Scotland!

MALCOLM: We shall not spend a large expense of time
     Before we reckon with your several loves
     And make us even with you. What's more to do
     Which could be planted newly with the time –
     As calling home our exiled friends abroad
     That fled the snares of watchful tyranny,
     Producing forth the cruel ministers
     Of this dead butcher and his fiend-like queen.
     So thanks to all at once and to each one,
     Whom we invite to see us crowned at Scone.

(*Flourish. They exit. Then immediately some of the actors cross
the stage, taking off costumes, etc., all a bit tired. As they exit:*)

r) *Broadway Theatre*

MACBETH (Forrest) *and* MACDUFF (Ryder) *enter fighting.*

MACREADY: Watch it. There. That's right. There.

     (*Then as* MACBETH.)

MACBETH: Before my body
     I throw my warlike shield. Lay on, Macduff;
     And damned be him that first cries, 'Hold, enough!'

(*They fight on stage. Finally at one point* MACBETH *is stabbed
and falls.* MACDUFF – *or rather* RYDER – *with some hesitation
raises his sword and appears to cut off* MACBETH's *head. A head
falls on the ground.* MACDUFF *picks it up. Others enter.*)

MACDUFF: (*With the head*) Hail, King of Scotland!

ALL: Hail, King of Scotland!

     (*Tableaux.*
     Blackout.)

SCENE 5

Projection: 5 p.m.

Forrest's dressing-room, the Broadway Theatre.
   Table, a couple of chairs, door. FORREST *sits, taking off his make-up; throughout the scene he changes from his Macbeth costume to his normal clothes.* RYDER, *still in costume, stands.*

FORREST: I don't know how this is any of my business.
RYDER: I think – The basis for the threats – or so Mr Macready believes – seems to be the fact that you are both performing the same play on the same – .
FORREST: So are you, Mr Ryder. (*Beat.*) So are you.
   (*Beat.*)
RYDER: On the same night. It's a competition that these people – whomever they are – are trying to . . . I don't know. Build up?
FORREST: According to Mr Macready.
RYDER: According to Mr – .
FORREST: This is what he has concluded.
RYDER: That's right. (*Beat.*) *I'm* only passing it along. I'm the messenger. That's all I am.
FORREST: I understand.
   (*Short pause.*)
RYDER: Anyway, a competition. English versus –
FORREST: You're English.
RYDER: I'm not saying that it's logical. (*Beat.*) English versus American. There is still, I suppose, a certain lingering – . Passion? It's uncorking this – , these tempers that has Mr Macready truly worried and why he believes there might be truth to the – .
FORREST: Do the threats mention me?
   (*Beat.*)
RYDER: No. Not in the letter I saw.
FORREST: So the basis for the threats actually remains in some doubt.
RYDER: They do criticize him for being foreign.

FORREST: I have been criticized in England for being foreign!
     (*Short pause.*)
     So they do not mention me. They do not mention that Mr
     Forrest happens, by coincidence, to be performing the
     same – .
RYDER: Mr Macready believes – .
FORREST: He has an opinion! (*Beat.*) And if I were Macready
     and I held such an opinion, the obvious action to take
     would be to change my schedule and perform something
     else.
RYDER: *He* can't.
FORREST: Too bad.
     (*Short pause.*)
     Then cancel.
     (*Knock at the door. Door opens,* TILTON *peeks in.*)
TILTON: Sorry about this afternoon, I . . .
FORREST: (*Continuing to* RYDER) But this is Mr Macready's
     business and it has nothing to do with me. (*Beat. To*
     TILTON) Sorry about what? What happened? Did
     something happen?
TILTON: I don't know where my mind was. It suddenly
     went . . .
FORREST: I don't know what you're talking about, Tilton.
     Please.
     (*Continues to undress. Beat.*)
TILTON: Thanks, Ned. Thank you. (TILTON *turns to go, bumps
     into* FISHER.) Sorry.
     (TILTON *leaves.*)
FISHER: You wanted to see me, Ned?
FORREST: Come in, Thomas, come in.
RYDER: Would you like me to – .
FORREST: Sit down, please. Both of you.(*Beat.*) I was just about
     to compliment Mr Ryder on his performance. After our
     little misfortune last night, we seem to have landed on our
     feet. (*Beat.*) Thanks to Mr Ryder.
FISHER: Nice work.
FORREST: (*Turns to* RYDER) You know I *have* seen you act
     before. In fact, I do believe I have seen you play this part

37

before. Now where was it? (*Beat.*) Could it have been in Edinburgh?

RYDER: I have played in – .

FORREST: I recall sneaking in one wet night to catch Mr Macready – .

RYDER: Yes, I did play Macduff to Mr Macready's – .

FORREST: But it was you whom I remember, Mr Ryder. (*Beat.*) I thought you were magnificent. The best Macduff I have ever seen.

RYDER: (*Smiles at* FISHER) Thank you.

FORREST: You see, most Macduffs don't realize that it is revenge that is driving the man. Passionate revenge. They don't show this. (*Beat.*) The part is not about Good triumphing. Who the hell knows if the man's good or not? It is hate that drives him. (*Beat.*) Ugly, sweaty hate. (*Beat.*) I hardly even remember the performance of the Macbeth.

RYDER: Mr Macready – .

FORREST: For that one night, the play should have been called *Macduff.*
(*Beat.*)

RYDER: (*Smiling*) Mr Forrest, I think you're putting me on. To call the play – .

FORREST: It would have been justified. By your performance. (*Beat.*) By your energetic and dominating performance. (*Short pause.*)
(*To himself*) *Macduff!* (*Beat.*) Macbeth need hardly even appear. (*Beat.*) What about a drink? The three of us? (*Takes a bottle and a few glasses.*)

RYDER: I don't really think – .

FORREST: I insist. Please.
(*Pause. He pours. Hands out glasses.*)
To you. And to our wonderful production which unfortunately we must call – *Macbeth.*
(*He drinks.* FISHER *laughs at the way* FORREST *is making his point with* RYDER.)
(*Turning quickly to* FISHER) Mr Fisher, you know we are scheduled to play here for the next five weeks.

FISHER: Of course I do, yes. Why do you – ?

38

FORREST: I ran into Mr Hackett the other day. Actually I believe it was just this morning. He said something about having engaged actors already for a tour. Do you know anything about this?

FISHER: I've met Hackett maybe two or three times in my whole life.

FORREST: I thought you worked for him once. I thought this is what you told me when I hired you for here.

FISHER: I worked for him. I did. (*Beat.*) But he wasn't around much.

FORREST: (*To* RYDER, *smiling*) It appears this tour is to be in – . What was the exact date? I forget. But I do remember it was about three and a half weeks from today. (*Beat.*) Or a week and a half before we finish our season here. (*Beat.*) You haven't talked to Mr Hackett about joining this tour, have you?

FISHER: That wouldn't be right, Ned.
(*Pause.*)

FORREST: I hear your brother hasn't been well.

FISHER: What do you mean? I don't have a – .

FORREST: So I'm sure there are a few unanticipated expenses. (*Beat.*) For the remainder of our season, I have decided to raise your pay by five dollars a performance. (*Beat.*) Rather, let's call it a bonus – to be collected at the end of our run.
(*Short pause.*)

FISHER: Thank you. I can use it. (*Beat.*) Is there anything else, you . . . ?

FORREST: No.
(FISHER *nods, puts down his glass and goes.*)
(*After he has closed the door*) You son of a bitch! (*To* RYDER) He's been in rehearsal for a week with Hackett. (*Beat.*) He's good though. Good with the sword.
(MISS BASS *enters, still in costume. She does not knock. In fact, throughout the rest of the scene, she undresses and changes into her normal clothes.* RYDER *takes notice of this, though for* FORREST *and* MISS BASS *it seems to be quite normal.*)

MISS BASS: (*While entering*) Can Helen come with us to the party?
(*Beat. Turns to* FORREST) Mr Robert Jones is taking Miss

Anne Holland to dinner tonight. So you can imagine how
Helen is feeling.

FORREST: I don't know how large the party's supposed to be.

MISS BASS: I can't leave her alone. I just got her to stop crying.

FORREST: Fine. (*Beat.*) Of course she can come. Maybe you, Mr
Ryder, would like to join . . .

RYDER: I'm having dinner with Mr Macready tonight. Otherwise
. . . (*Short pause.*) I'll tell him I passed along his message. I
should go. (*Goes to the door.*) By the way, thank you for last
night. It was a pleasure to – And I am pleased you like my
Macduff. I'm a bit more critical of it than you though.
(*Beat.*) I think I should try to, I don't know. I just think I
could be subtler. After all, the play Shakespeare wrote isn't
called *Macduff*, is it?
(*Forces himself to laugh, and he leaves. Long pause.* FORREST
begins to get dressed.)

MISS BASS: I've heard that there are quite a few unsold tickets for
Mr Macready's *Macbeth*.

FORREST: (*Without looking up*) Is that true?
(*Laughs to himself.*)

MISS BASS: Why is that . . . ?
(*He looks up, shakes his head, suddenly sits and sighs. She looks
at him.*)

MISS BASS: (*Trying to be bright*) So where's the party?

FORREST: New York Hotel.

MISS BASS: You're sure they won't mind us bringing Helen . . . ?

FORREST: I'm sure it's a big party. That's what I remember my
wife saying at least.

MISS BASS: The bigger the better. For us.
(*Pause.* FORREST *slowly turns to her.*)

MISS BASS: What? What?

FORREST: My wife doesn't want you in our house any more. She
made this clear to me. This morning. (*Beat.*) Do you mind?

MISS BASS: Then – she's not welcome in mine either.
(*Beat. She smiles.*)

FORREST: (*Sigh of relief*) Thank you. You make this much easier.
(*He smiles but then begins nearly to cry.*)

MISS BASS: Ned . . . ?

FORREST: I don't know what it is, Jane. (*Beat.*) For no reason my
eyes start to well up. (*He wipes his tears, breathes deeply,
sighs.*) Life's not half as much fun as theatre.
(*He continues to get dressed.
Blackout.*)

SCENE 6

Projection: 8 p.m.

A private drawing room, New York Hotel.
  MACREADY, RYDER, MRS FORREST, DION BOUCICAULT *and
his wife* AGNES, *in the middle of conversation.*

MACREADY: He said she was fifty if she was anything, and when
she finished, she told Johnstone that her parts include not
only Desdemona but also Juliet. (*Smiles and shakes his head,
sips his drink. Others smile as well.*) Then in Pittsburg – a town
he said one should be lucky enough to avoid – he's to play
Lear with a Goneril who never was sober – for four days, he
swears – a Cordelia who not only talked nonsense, as if she
had concluded that nonsense was Shakespeare's intention
and she was only clarifying this point, but who also was a
good three to four years older than him, and John Johnstone,
well you've seen him.
MRS FORREST: Not for years, has he . . . ?
MACREADY: (*Turns to* BOUCICAULT) He's – . What? How would
you describe . . . ?
BOUCICAULT: No one would say he was too young for the part.
Of Lear.
MACREADY: It happened rather quickly as well.
AGNES: His son died.
MACREADY: Is that it? I didn't know.
(*Short pause.*)
BOUCICAULT: So his Cordelia was even older than – .
MACREADY: Which he said actually made the relationship rather
interesting.

41

BOUCICAULT: It's different.

MACREADY: Anyway, he finally just felt that the performance he was giving was just too good for them. They cheered, of course, but he was convinced they didn't know what in the world they were cheering for.

(*Short pause.*)

BOUCICAULT: Hmmmm. (*Turns to look at* AGNES *for a moment, then turns to* RYDER.) Mr Ryder, has this been your experience of – ?

RYDER: No. (*Beat.*) Actually it hasn't. I think Americans – .

MACREADY: (*Interrupting*) Nor has it been mine, Mr Boucicault. American people are really rather charming and decent as well as intelligent in an instinctive sort of way. The actors I am working with, they may not know certain things, things you or I or your wife might take for granted, but that doesn't mean they aren't quick to learn.

AGNES: Being married to an American, Mrs Forrest, you must have had experiences.

MRS FORREST: Oh yes. Very many.

(*Pause. They look to her to continue.*)

MACREADY: (*Finally*) Not only are they quick to learn, they are eager. They're more like children than us old jaded English actors. (*Laughs lightly, as do others.*) It's a fascinating country, it truly is!

AGNES: Whatever it is, it at least sounds somewhat refreshing after the London theatre.

RYDER: Absolutely nothing was happening there when we left.

BOUCICAULT: And it's got worse, hasn't it?

(*Turns to* AGNES, *who nods.*)

Kean's made a complete mess of the Princess.

AGNES: (*To the others*) Not a complete – .

BOUCICAULT: He has, it's true. (*Beat.*) I gave him *The Corsican Brothers* – for nothing – for nearly nothing he has the play of the century. What is clearly my best play; what is going to be my most successful play that will make *London Assurance* seem like . . . Whatever. (*Beat.*) Crowds fight to get into my play. This play cannot lose money (*Turns to* AGNES.) He ran it for what – ?

AGNES: Not long enough.

BOUCICAULT: I try to tell him. (*Shakes his head.*) What is in it for me? I don't get a pound more if he plays the play or not. Not there. At the Princess he can play it forever and I don't get a farthing more. (*Beat.*) It's going to be done here. (*Beat.*) Last night Hackett agreed to take it.

MACREADY: When did he say – ?

BOUCICAULT: Some time after the new year. He didn't give me dates. (*Beat.*) But it's definite. (*Beat.*) We're going to work out a deal. (*Beat. Laughs*) We're here one week and – ! I love America. (*Short pause.*)

AGNES: (*Smiling*) Hopefully we're saying the same thing next week. (*Beat.*) At first we were very happy with Kean.

BOUCICAULT: I never was, Agnes. It was the Princess Theatre that I loved. A beautiful theatre.

MACREADY: This is true.

BOUCICAULT: What does Kean replace my play with? *Twelfth Night.* He insists on doing this play. (*Beat.*) It's not a bad play. (*Beat.*) But I tell him just run the goddamn *Corsican Brothers* until no one comes any more. Does this sound mad?!

AGNES: Dion – .

BOUCICAULT: Let me finish! (*Beat.*) It's as if they don't want to make money. (*Beat.*) It is exactly as if they don't want to make money!!
(*Pause.*)

RYDER: That is very good news about Hackett.

AGNES: He's going to tell us for sure next week.
(*Short pause.*)

BOUCICAULT: Have any of you been to Cincinnati?

MRS FORREST: Cincinnati? (*Looks at the others.*) No, I haven't.

MACREADY: No. (*Beat.*) Why? Is there something . . . ?

BOUCICAULT: It's just that I always have loved that name: Cincinnati.
(*Pause: they sip their drinks.*)

MACREADY: Five Brits all in one room. In America. That doesn't happen very often.

MRS FORREST: Yes it does.
(*Pause.*)

43

AGNES: We've reserved a small table in the dining-room. As soon as Mr Forrest . . .

MRS FORREST: I think it might be dangerous to wait for my husband.

(*Short pause.*)

BOUCICAULT: Perhaps then we should go right to our table. We can bring our drinks.

(*They hesitate.*)

AGNES: We should leave a message at the front desk.

RYDER: He may have forgotten. Maybe there was something else.

MRS FORREST: Do you know if Mr Forrest has gone somewhere else?

RYDER: No. (*Beat.*) I don't know anything.

MRS FORREST: I'll leave the note.

BOUCICAULT: We'll just be – .

MRS FORREST: Yes.

(*As the others move off towards the dining-room:*)

BOUCICAULT: So you're staying here as well?

MACREADY: It's near the theatre.

AGNES: They've been very nice to us.

MACREADY: (*To* AGNES) Here, let me carry your drink.

AGNES: Thank you.

(*They are gone.* MRS FORREST *has watched them go; she sighs and sits. After a moment she stands again and turns to go off towards the front desk just as* FORREST *enters with* MISS BASS *and* MISS BURTON. FORREST *stops. Short pause.*)

FORREST: Where's the party?

MRS FORREST: What party are you talking about? And where have you been?

FORREST: Boucicault's party. You told me tonight was Boucicault's party. We've been looking all over the hotel . . .

MRS FORREST: It's not a party. It's a dinner, Mr Forrest. A small dinner.

(*Short pause.*)

FORREST: Then I made a mistake.

MISS BASS: If you want us to go, Ned . . .

FORREST: Where's the dinner?

MRS FORREST: (*Nods*) Through there.

44

(*Beat.*)

FORREST: What's a few more places? (*Tries to laugh.*) They're through there?
(*She does not respond. He hesitates, then leads the women in the direction of the dining-room.*)

MRS FORREST: Edwin.
(*He stops.*)

FORREST: (*To* BASS *and* BURTON) I'll join you in a minute. Just introduce yourselves. It'll be fine. (*Beat.*) It's fine.
(*They go. Short pause.*)

MRS FORREST: What have you been doing?

FORREST: Rehearsing.

MRS FORREST: What have you been doing?

FORREST: One of the girls, Miss Burton; she's upset because her boyfriend – the boy she thinks is her boyfriend . . . (*Beat.*) You know who I mean. (*Beat.*) My Banquo. Well, tonight he's taken another actress, Miss – .

MRS FORREST: Why do I care? How could you invite them?

FORREST: They're actresses in my – ! (*He stops himself. Short pause.*) I made a mistake. I am sorry. (*Beat.*) I invited them to what I thought was – . I can't tell them to leave. (*Beat.*) It would be profoundly embarrassing to just . . . (*Beat.*) Let's just get through this, Catherine.
(*The others all return from the dining-room.*)

AGNES: (*Entering*) No, it's my fault really for not reserving a larger table.

MRS FORREST: What's – ?

MACREADY: We don't all fit around the table.

BOUCICAULT: And they said they can't add on – The space in there, there's no – .
(*Beat.*)

AGNES: They're seeing what they can do. They asked us to wait.
(*Awkward pause.*)

FORREST: I'm sorry if I caused any trouble.

AGNES: Of course not. We're very pleased and honoured you could come. And your guests. We're very anxious to get to know all sorts of Americans.

FORREST: Thank you.

45

AGNES: Aren't we?

BOUCICAULT: We are. (*Beat.*) We certainly are.

(*Another awkward pause.*)

AGNES: I'll see if anything's been figured out yet.

(*She goes. Short pause.*)

FORREST: Mr Boucicault, it is very nice to see you again. I hope your voyage was comfortable.

(*They shake hands.*)

BOUCICAULT: Very. Thank you. You of course know Mr Macready.

FORREST: We've met before. How do you do?

MACREADY: How do you do?

BOUCICAULT: And Mr Ryder.

FORREST: Mr Ryder is my Macduff at the moment actually.

BOUCICAULT: Really? I didn't – You didn't say anything.

MACREADY: I have an American Macduff for New York. I thought it a good thing. (*Beat.*) He's very good as well.

(*Short pause.*)

RYDER: Funny, Mr Forrest, you asked me what I was doing this evening – . I guess you were going to invite me here. And here I am already. (*Laughs lightly.*) With Mr Macready. (*Beat.*) I told you I was having dinner with Mr Macready.

MRS FORREST: My husband invited you as well?

(*Pause.*)

FORREST: (*To* MISS BASS) You've been introduced, I – .

MISS BASS: Actually . . .

(*She shakes her head.*)

MISS BURTON: No, we – .

AGNES: I'm terribly sorry.

FORREST: Miss Burton. Miss Bass.

(*An exchange of polite greetings. Short pause.*)

They are two of my witches.

(*The others nod as if this explains something.*)

MISS BURTON: I'm the second.

MISS BASS: I'm the first.

(AGNES *enters, followed by a maid and a servant carrying tables.*)

AGNES: (*While entering*) They think we'll actually be more

46

comfortable in here. We'll set up to eat in here. And we can add on as many tables as we wish. (*Beat.*) In case others should drop in. (*Beat.*) I do love it when people feel they can just drop in. (*Beat.*) For dinner.

(*During much of the scene, the tables are set up, then set with tablecloths, plates, glasses, etc.*)

BOUCICAULT: I hear wonderful things about your *Macbeth*, Mr Forrest. (*Beat.*) Or should I say, all of your *Macbeth*, as it seems half of your cast is with us tonight.

FORREST: Thank you. (*Short pause.*) And let's not leave Mr Macready out. *His Macbeth* I have seen! Where was it? I was just today telling Mr Ryder. Baltimore? Cincinnati?

BOUCICAULT: Agnes – Cincinnati.

(*She nods and smiles.*)

RYDER: It was Edinburgh.

MACREADY: I hadn't known. Had I known – .

FORREST: You were . . . Unforgettable. Even now I can close my eyes and see you there. (*Beat.*) As Macbeth. (*Beat.*) Unforgettable.

BOUCICAULT: Yes. And yours, it's on everyone's lips.

FORREST: What brings you to New York, Mr Boucicault?

MACREADY: He's sold his *Corsican Brothers* to Hackett. They're doing it next year.

FORREST: I hope you got the money in your hand. He'll promise anything.

(BOUCICAULT *looks at* AGNES.)

AGNES: My husband has a new play.

FORREST: What's the title – ?

BOUCICAULT: I don't want to bother you two – . (*Beat.*) Actually, now that I think of it you both could be of some help to me. That's if you don't mind. I wouldn't want you to think you had to work for your dinner.

(*Laughs. No one else does.*)

AGNES: I think we can sit down.

BOUCICAULT: Please, let's – . (*Gestures for all to go to the table.*) The play is called *Shakespeare in Love*.

RYDER: Who's sitting where?

AGNES: Dion should be at the head. Then Miss – .

47

MISS BURTON: Burton.

AGNES: Burton to his left. And who – ? Mr Forrest? Or would you rather sit by your wife?

FORREST: I don't care where I sit.

BOUCICAULT: And it's about Shakespeare.

AGNES: I'll sit at the other end. Mr Ryder, then . . .

(*She points to where he should sit.*)

MRS FORREST: Then I'll sit there.

(*Goes to her seat.*)

BOUCICAULT: And he is in love. Shakespeare.

AGNES: Then Mr Macready.

MACREADY: Where?

AGNES: Right here, next to Dion and Mrs Forrest.

BOUCICAULT: He's in love with a neighbour.

MACREADY: How old is he?

BOUCICAULT: He's in his late thirties I would say. Though that could be changed. (*Beat.*) He can be older. He can be younger.

AGNES: And that leaves Miss Bass. Miss Bass on the other side of Mr Forrest. Who has Miss Burton on one side and Miss Bass on the other.

MRS FORREST: My husband will be in heaven.

AGNES: Shall we sit?

(*They do. There is no food or drink on the table.*)

BOUCICAULT: It's a comedy. A rather fantastical comedy. Because, you see, various characters from his plays come back to him – to try to help him or they are just plain jealous of this love affair and are feeling neglected. They are very unhappy that this affair is upsetting their lives. (*Beat.*) It's a very good idea, isn't it?

AGNES: Dion, they aren't serving the food. Maybe they've forgotten about us.

BOUCICAULT: Why would they . . . ? (*He gets up.*) I'll go and see. Excuse me. Remind me where I was.

(*He goes. Short pause.*)

AGNES: It's nice in here. (*Beat.*) To have a whole room by yourself. (*Beat.*) Things do work out.

FORREST: Mr Macready, Mr Ryder was telling me about some

threats against . . . (*Turns to* RYDER.) Who exactly were they against?

MACREADY: Threats?

RYDER: About Monday. About the two *Macbeth*s.

MACREADY: Threats??

RYDER: About being foreign. The letters you received.

MACREADY: Threats???

RYDER: You asked me to talk to Mr Forrest and – .

MACREADY: Oh those. Silly ridiculous rumours. I'm sure the same must happen to you, Mr Forrest. Jealous people.

FORREST: In England it happens to me all the time.

    (*Beat.*)

MACREADY: One learns to ignore such things.

    (*Short pause.*)

FORREST: You're selling very well, I hear.

    (*Short pause.*)

MRS FORREST: They don't like English people.

FORREST: Who are they?

    (*She shrugs.*)

    You don't know what you're talking about.

    (*She looks down, puts her head in her hands.*)

AGNES: Do you like English people, Miss . . .

MISS BURTON: Burton. Sure. (*She smiles.*) What's not to like.

    (*Beat.*) What's *to* like? People are people. (*Shrugs.*) There are good and there are bad.

    (MISS BASS *smiles.*)

    What's funny?

MISS BASS: Nothing.

MISS BURTON: You're laughing at me.

MISS BASS: I'm not, Helen.

AGNES: What you say is true.

RYDER: Very true.

    (*Beat.*)

AGNES: Dion doesn't like English people, but then he's Irish.

MACREADY: By the way, except for the accent, you'd hardly notice. He's very well groomed.

AGNES: I don't think I will tell him that.

MISS BASS: Why wouldn't I like you, Mrs Forrest? (*Beat.*) Just

because you're English?
(*Pause.*)

MRS FORREST: I wasn't talking about you. I wasn't talking to
you. (*Turns to* AGNES.) The women, you'll find, it will shock
you, Agnes. No – subtlety. No – charm, that I can see. So of
course they will do anything. Anything. (*Shakes her head.*)
Sometimes for nothing, sometimes they want to be paid for
it. (*Turns to* FORREST.) Isn't that right?

FORREST: Catherine.

MRS FORREST: The men are much more subtle. No, perhaps
subtle is the wrong word. (*Beat.*) Tricky. This is the word.
They can be very very . . .
(*Short pause.*)
(*Without looking at anyone*) My apologies. To all of you.
Including Miss Burton and Miss Bass. (*Beat.*) I promise you,
I do not normally act in this manner.
(*Beat.* BOUCICAULT *comes back in, followed by a servant with
the food.*)

BOUCICAULT: I don't know what they were waiting for. Anyway,
I was talking about my play. (*Beat.*) A very nice idea, isn't it?
Shakespeare in love. So who should play Shakespeare? (*He
has sat back down.*) That seems to be the question. (*Beat.*)
You both know actors. On both sides of the ocean. Who
would be good to play our greatest dramatist? (*Beat. To* MISS
BURTON) I'm having a reading next week. In the afternoon
so all of you busy theatre actors can come. (*Beat.*) The
reading isn't completely cast yet. (*Beat.*) Any ideas about
who could play Shakespeare? Not in the reading. I'll play
him in the reading. (*Beat.*) He'd have to be a major actor.
Think about it. (*Suddenly laughs.*) But as I said – I don't want
you to think you have to work for your dinner. (*Laughs.
Stops. Looks at the food.*) This looks good.
(*Blackout.*)

Projection: 1 a.m.

The same. The dinner is long over, though the dishes remain on the table, as well as wine bottles, glasses, etc.
    MRS FORREST *and* AGNES *have left some time earlier.* FORREST, *with* MISS BASS *at his side, sits at the table and talks to* MACREADY, *who has his head on the table, and occasionally to* BOUCICAULT, *who sits next to* MISS BURTON *and at times turns and stares at her and smiles.* RYDER *is out for a pee.*

FORREST: I'm serious. I think what one must do – . What the
    battle finally is about. For us. You need to – . With your
    hands out – keeping it all away – . All out of the way. (*Beat.*)
    Everything that is coming at you. The distractions and
    everything. Everything like that. Out there. The moment
    you go off the stage it is like – to me, I feel this – it is like they
    are trying to take it all away from you. (*Beat.*) Tell you it
    never happened. What you felt out there on the stage! What
    you knew you had done out there on the stage!
    (*Short pause.*)
MISS BURTON: (*To* BOUCICAULT) Will you stop smiling at me!
    (*He smiles and takes a sip of wine.*)
FORREST: They may mean well. These people. Well-wishers
    mean well, but – . (*Beat.*) Sometimes I think it's all just
    interference. And the test we are putting ourselves through
    . . . Have been put through – . By whom? Where does it
    come from? God? I don't know. But it's to push all that
    away. Not let it break into the art of what we do.
    (*Short pause.*)
MACREADY: (*Lifts up his head for a moment*) The world should be
    left behind. In the dressing-room.
FORREST: It certainly should not be brought on to the stage.
    (*Beat. To* MISS BASS) You don't agree.
MISS BASS: I didn't say any – .
FORREST: Take an argument you might have. With – ? Anyone.
    A friend. (*Beat.*) A wife. You have this argument.

51

You're boiling over. Then you must play Hamlet. If you try to bring that argument into – . On to – . (*Beat*.) You have to push it all away. Become someone who has not had an argument. In this case who does not have a wife.

MACREADY: (*Lifting head*) And into someone whose father just died.

FORREST: Exactly.

(*Beat*.)

MACREADY: Now if my father *had* just died and I *had* to play Hamlet that night – .

FORREST: This I would love to see.

MACREADY: That would be – . (*Beat*.) Yes.

(*He smiles*.)

FORREST: (*Smiling*) But fathers don't die every time we play Hamlet. (*Beat*.) Instead, bills are sent that day which can be wrong. You step in horse shit on the street. Wives don't listen when you talk to them. You lose your favourite pen. Or hat. Or your right shoe. Or other stocking. (*Beat*.) Or you fall in love that day. Or hear a joke that you cannot forget and cannot stop smiling about. Your brother writes and says he's going to visit. The breakfast wasn't at all what you wanted. (*Beat*.) And then you play Hamlet. Then you become someone else. (*Beat*.) To do this you must learn to forget. (*Takes a sip of wine*.) Sometimes I think this is my favourite part of being an actor.

(*Pause*. RYDER *enters and sits*.)

RYDER: What did I miss?

(MACREADY, *without picking up his head, just shakes his head*.)

BOUCICAULT: (*Standing up, to* RYDER) Good idea. I have to go too. (*He leans over and tries to kiss* MISS BURTON, *who slaps him hard across the head. Others turn and see this*. BOUCICAULT *smiles and leaves*.)

MACREADY: (*With head down*) For me I think I like being able to – It's not: forget. But I know what you mean.

MISS BURTON: (*Standing*) I think I should be leaving, it's – .

MISS BASS: Helen, it's only – .

MISS BURTON: He's climbing all over me. That's not what I came for!

52

At left, Victor Garber as Edwin Forrest with Brian Bedford as
William Charles Macready.

From left to right, Judy Kuhn as Helen Burton, Victor Garber
as Edwin Forrest, Jennifer Van Dyck as Jane Bass, Laura
Innes as Agnes Robertson, Zeljko Ivanek as John Ryder,
Frances Conroy as Catherine Forrest and Brian Bedford as
William Charles Macready.

From left to right, Alan Brasington as Charles Clark, LeClanché Du Rand as Mrs. Pope, Bill Moor as Frederick Wemyss, Michael Butler as George Bradshaw, Brian Bedford as William Charles Macready, Tim MacDonald as James Bridges and Tom Aldredge as Washington Irving.

From left to right, Brian Bedford,
Zeljko Ivanek and Victor Garber.

FORREST: Sit over here with us. We'll make room.

MISS BASS: I'll move over.

FORREST: Come on. Come on. We won't stay much longer.
(*She sits next to* MISS BASS, *protected from* BOUCICAULT *by both* FORREST *and* RYDER. *They move a chair for her.*)

MACREADY: (*Finally*) As I was saying – .

FORREST: (*To* MISS BURTON) We're talking about why we act. What we – . Why do you act?

MISS BURTON: I don't know.
(*He looks at her and nods. He turns back to* MACREADY.)

MACREADY: It's hard to explain really. Where shall I begin?
(*Beat.*) You see – as Descartes has said – inside us all are these – . He called them animal spirits. (*Beat.*) Which are really, what other people call – passions.
(*Short pause.* FORREST *nods.*)
And they're all – these spirits – they're bordered, they're all sort of fenced in. (*Suddenly remembering*) You could also call them *emotions*. (*Beat.*) Anyway, they're fenced in. But when one of them escapes from the others – . And is not quickly caught by – . I don't know, spirits who do the catching, like sheep-dogs catch – .
(*Beat.*)

FORREST: Sheep.

MACREADY: That's right. Like sheep-dogs catch sheep. Anyway, when one escapes and it not caught, then it becomes a very deep, a very – . A very passionate – . (*Beat.*) What?! (*Beat. Remembers.*) Feeling! Feeling. (*Short pause.*) So what an actor does – I believe – is this: philosophically speaking – . I haven't studied enough philosophy – . I'd like to study much much more, but – . Well – . People like us who are busy *doing* – ! But, as I was saying, the art of the actor – . (*Beat.*) What was I going to say? I was about to say something that was very clear. I remember. The art of the actor is like ripping down the fences. (*Beat.*) And tying up the sheep-dogs. (*Beat.*) And letting the spirits loose. A few at a time. Or more! Depending on the part. Letting them roam for a while. (*Short pause.*) So, that's what I love about acting. (*Pause.*) I don't know how clear I've been.

53

FORREST: No, no, you've been . . . (*Nods and shrugs.*)

(BOUCICAULT *had entered while* MACREADY *was talking. He has noticed that* MISS BURTON *has moved and has hesitated, not knowing where he should now sit. He brings a chair, trying to squeeze in next to* MISS BURTON.)

MISS BURTON: There's no room here.

MACREADY: Dion, stay over there.

BOUCICAULT: There's no one over there.

(*He stands behind her, making her very uncomfortable.*)

FORREST: (*To* MACREADY) That was very interesting.

MACREADY: I've only tried to explain it to one other person, and he laughed so – . (*Shrugs.*) You can see how I might be a little – . About talking about . . .

FORREST: Please! (*Beat.*) Please, we are all actors here.

MISS BASS: (*Stands up.*) I'll sit over there.

(*She moves to where* MISS BURTON *had been sitting and* BOUCICAULT *follows, going back to his seat.*)

FORREST: (*To* MACREADY) No one would make fun . . .

RYDER: (*To* MACREADY) What's that on your sleeve? Don't move, I'll kill it. (*He goes to get something off Macready's jacket.*) I got it! Oh my God, it's an escaped animal spirit! Quick, kill it! Kill it! Kill it!

(*He laughs at his joke,* MACREADY *and* FORREST *ignore him.*)

MACREADY: It's a theory. A way of talking about something that is not easy to talk about.

(FORREST *nods.*)

BOUCICAULT: In my play, *Shakespeare in Love*, Shakespeare, by falling in love, can't write. Or doesn't want to write. (*Beat.*) His talent dies. This is why the characters from his plays – .

MACREADY: I thought we finished talking about your play, Dion.

BOUCICAULT: Had we? I'm sorry, I didn't know.

(*Short pause.*)

(*Turns to* MISS BASS.) Which witch (*Through his drunkenness he has trouble saying this*) – Which witch do you play? May I ask? (*Beat.*) In *Macbeth*.

MISS BASS: I'm the first witch.

BOUCICAULT: Ah, the first one. Mmmmmmmm. Not the one I would have chosen for you, but a good one just the same.

54

MACREADY: (*Standing with difficulty*) I have no more to say. So I
   am going to bed.
   (RYDER *stands, then* FORREST.)
FORREST: (*To the women*) I shall take you two home.
BOUCICAULT: Wait a minute! What about my problem? How
   shall I choose between you on Monday night? Whose
   Macbeth do I attend?
FORREST: It doesn't matter to – .
BOUCICAULT: Perhaps I shall have to flip a coin. Who has a coin?
   I have a coin. (*Beat.*) Ready? Heads and I go to Mr – .
   Forrest's. And tails to Mr Macready's. (*Flips and the coin
   falls under the table.*) I will get it. No one move. I am getting
   it.
   (*The others stand and watch as* BOUCICAULT *crawls under the
   table.*)
   I can't – . Did anyone see which way it rolled? (*Bumps his
   head.*) Ow!
   (He grabs MISS BURTON'*s ankle.*)
MISS BURTON: Stop that! (*She kicks him, he laughs.*) Get me out
   of here.
MISS BASS: We're going. Ned?
FORREST: It is late.
BOUCICAULT: I have it! I found it! (*Comes out from under the
   table.*) Here it is. (*Looks at the coin.*) I forget. Who had tails
   and who had heads?
   (*Others immediately move to leave, ignoring* BOUCICAULT.)
FORREST: Mr Ryder, I shall see you on Monday.
RYDER: I'll be there.
MISS BASS: Can we drop you off somewhere?
RYDER: I have rooms here in the hotel.
MISS BASS: So you don't have far – .
RYDER: No.
MISS BASS: They're comfortable rooms I hope.
FORREST: Do you want him to show you them?
MISS BASS: Ned!
FORREST: I didn't mean – . (*Turns to* BOUCICAULT.) Mr
   Boucicault, I thank you for this evening.
MACREADY: Yes, a lovely affair.

55

BOUCICAULT: Is everyone leaving?

MISS BURTON: We are.

FORREST: Mr Macready, we have a cab.

MACREADY: I'm staying in the hotel as well.

FORREST: Ah. (*Leaving*) Helen. Jane.

MACREADY: (*Leaving*) So – I'm home.

BOUCICAULT: (*Leaving*) Thank you for coming. (*To* MISS
BURTON) It was charming to meet you.
(*In the distance, we hear them say 'goodnight' and they are gone.
Blackout.*)

SCENE 8

Projection: Three days later, Monday 7 May. 7.30 p.m.

Backstage, Astor Place Opera House.
*A curtain, upstage of which is the stage and audience. On this stage,
through the curtain, in silhouette,* Act I scene iii *of* Macbeth *is being
performed by the* THREE WITCHES (Sefton, Chippindale *and*
Bridges). *Backstage someone makes the thunder-sound.*
*Downstage of this curtain, actors in costume and not, listen, wait
and mill around. After a moment, one actor with a drum bangs on it,
and from 'the stage' one vaguely hears:*

3RD WITCH: A drum! a drum!
Macbeth doth come.

ALL: The Weird Sisters, hand in hand,
Posters of the sea and land,
Thus do go about, about:
Thrice to thine, and thrice to mine,
And thrice again, to make up nine.
Peace! – The charm's wound up.
(*Backstage,* MACREADY *dressed in costume has entered. He slaps*
BRADSHAW [Banquo] *on the back, and* BRADSHAW *enters 'on
stage'. From the audience, one hears cheers and yells.*
MACREADY *smiles.*)

MACREADY: (*To the actor with the drum*) They think he's me.

(*He makes his entrance.*)
So foul and fair day I have not seen.
(*Before he can even get the sentence out, boos and cries ring out from the audience, then screaming and yells and violent insults. The other actors look at each other. From the stage,* BANQUO *is heard trying to go on, as do the* WITCHES, *but all is chaos. Finally,* MACREADY *can be heard screaming:*)
Stay, you imperfect speakers, tell me more!
(*But he is drowned out. Suddenly someone rips down the curtain, and* MACREADY's *face is seen to be completely bloodied; he staggers back, ducking the things being thrown at him. Other actors run for cover.* MACREADY *stumbles and turns to an actor.*)
Who are they? What do they want?!
(*The* WITCHES *hurry in* [Sefton, Chippindale *and* Bridges].)
MRS POPE: (*Taking* MACREADY) Sit down. Over here. Let me get you a cloth.
(*She takes him to a chair.*)
BRIDGES: He's bleeding.
MACREADY: They tried to kill me! (*Grabs* CHIPPINDALE.) They want to kill me!
CHIPPINDALE: (*Taking the cloth from* MRS POPE) Give me that. Let me wipe your face.
(MACREADY *screams.*)
MACREADY: I haven't done anything to them. They have interrupted my performance!
(*He stands.*)
MRS POPE: Sit down.
(*The yelling and screaming continue from the audience.*)
BRADSHAW: (*Entering from the stage*) They're breaking the seats.
CHIPPINDALE: Get them to stop.
MACREADY: Shoot them! Shoot them!
SEFTON: Tell them he's left the theatre. Tell them he's gone.
MACREADY: I haven't left. I am here!
(*He stands.*)
CHIPPINDALE: Get them to stop!
(*Beat.* SEFTON *hurries off to the 'stage'.*)
MACREADY: I must finish!

SEFTON: (*Off, to the audience, yelling*) Mr Macready has left the theatre!

MACREADY: I need to finish!

SEFTON: (*Off*) Mr Macready has left the theatre!

(*Yelling and screaming continue. Pause.* MACREADY, *in the chair, suddenly realizes that all the other actors are now looking at him.*)

SEFTON: (*Off*) Macready has left the theatre!

(*Beat. Screaming dies down and suddenly there is a deafening cheer from the audience.*

Blackout.)

ACT TWO

SCENE I

Projection: The next day, Tuesday 8 May. 9.45 p.m.

The stage of the Broadway Theatre during a performance of
Metamora. FORREST *as the title character and* MISS HOLLAND *as
Metamora's wife,* NAHMEOKEE. *The last few minutes of the play.*

METAMORA: Nahmeokee, I look up through the long path of thin
air, and I think I see our infant borne onward to the land of
the happy, where the fair hunting grounds know no storms
or snows, and where the immortal brave feast in the eyes of
the giver of good. Look upwards, Nahmeokee, the spirit of
thy murdered father beckons thee.

NAHMEOKEE: I will go to him.

METAMORA: Embrace me, Nahmeokee – 'twas like the first you
gave me in the days of our strength and joy – they are gone.
(*Places his ear to the ground.*) Hark! In the distant wood I
faintly hear the cautious tread of men! They are upon us,
Nahmeokee – the home of the happy is made ready for thee.
(*He stabs her, she dies.*) She felt no white man's bondage –
free as the air she lived – pure as the snow she died! In smiles
she died! Let me taste it, ere her lips are cold as the ice.
(*Loud shouts. Roll of drums.* KAWESHINE (Fisher) *leads*
CHURCH (Tilton) *and* SOLDIERS.)

CHURCH: He is found! Metamora is our prisoner.

METAMORA: No! He lives – last of his race – but still your enemy
– lives to defy you still. Though numbers overpower me and
treachery surrounds me, though friends desert me, I defy
you still! Come to me – come singly to me! And this true
knife that has tasted the foul blood of your nation and now is
red with the purest of mine, will feel a gasp as strong as when
it flashed in the blaze of your burning buildings, or was lifted
terribly over the fallen in battle.

CHURCH: Fire upon him!

METAMORA: Do so, I am weary of the world for ye are dwellers in

59

it; I would not turn upon my heel to save my life.
CHURCH: Your duty, soldiers.
(*They fire.* METAMORA *falls.*)
METAMORA: My curses on you, white men! May the Great Spirit
curse you when he speaks in his war voice from the clouds!
Murderers! The last of the Wampanoags' curse be on you!
May your graves and the graves of your children be in the
path the red man shall trace! And may the wolf and panther
howl o'er your fleshless bones, fit banquet for the destroyers!
Spirits of the grave, I come! But the curse of Metamora stays
with the white man! I die! My wife! My Queen! My
Nahmeokee!
(*Falls and dies. A tableau is formed. Drums and trumpet sound a
retreat. Slow curtain.
Blackout.*)

SCENE 2

Projection: 10 p.m.

Macready's rooms, New York Hotel.
*The actors from the Astor Place Opera House production of Macbeth
– including* CLARK, MRS POPE, WEMYSS, BRIDGES, BRADSHAW,
SEFTON, CHIPPINDALE, *and* ARNOLD – *stand about, some have
drinks in hand – as an elderly man,* WASHINGTON IRVING, *tries to
address them.*

IRVING: (*Straining a little*) I can only assure you all that it is the
firm conclusion of those in positions to know in this city that
the real cause of last night's attack at the Astor Place Opera
House had absolutely nothing to do with you or with
Mr Macready.
MRS POPE: That's nice to know, but –.
IRVING: You were neither the real target nor in any way the true
provocation of what transpired.
CLARK: Then who were – ?
IRVING: Explanations are being sought at this very minute by

60

those who know far more than us. (*Tries to smile.*) Please, trust this. Put what occurred last night into the past. This is all we ask. (*Beat.*) I am here only to recommend that we all leave the politics to the politicians.

CLARK: (*To* WEMYSS) He won't have to twist my –.

IRVING: And to guarantee – to all of you – your complete safety during a second performance of Mr Macready's *Macbeth*. (*The actors are shocked, and all speak at once:* 'What?!' 'That's madness!' 'Who's going to perform it?!' 'Once was enough.' *etc.*)
(*Shouting*) Mr Macready –! Please! Mr Macready has been persuaded . . .!
(*The actors quieten down.*)
Been persuaded that there is no significant risk.
(*Beat.*)
For him.
(*Beat.*)
And for those who wish to join him on the stage.

ARNOLD: Is that why we were asked to come . . .?
(*Stops himself as* MACREADY, *looking tired and somewhat dazed, enters from his bedroom. Others look at him.*
IRVING *smiles at* MACREADY, *pats him gingerly on the back and continues.*)

IRVING: A delegation of citizens – leading citizens, I hasten to add, met this morning. It is to these men that I have already referred.
(*Beat.*)
I was honoured to be counted among their number. One conclusion of this meeting was the designation of a person to express for all a deep apology to Mr Macready. And to you other actors as well. (*Short pause. Then he laughs.*) I told them I was probably the worst person for this job. I told them – you probably had never even heard of me. (*Laughs. No one else does.*) Of Washington Irving.

ARNOLD: I didn't realize that's who he –.

MRS POPE: Sh-sh.

IRVING: But I was assured. (*Smiles.*) I suppose they thought as one artist to . . . (*Shrugs.*) Most of the committee of course are not – . Though that's not to say they do not appreciate art. And artists. They've been very good to me. (*Laughs to himself. Everyone just looks at him.*) Anyway, I agreed. As I was also eager to pay my own respects for the courage shown by all of you last night. For this I applaud you all. (*He applauds lightly. No one else does.*) And it is out of this admiration for your strengths and courage that I am confident to ask you all to consider performing another –.

MRS POPE: Were you there last night?

IRVING: Unfortunately, I was not. But I have heard –.

BRADSHAW: They wanted to kill –.

IRVING: If Mr Macready is convinced –.

CLARK: It seems a risk . . .

IRVING: (*Suddenly turns on them with surprising vehemence*) Of course it's a risk!!! There's risk in any important endeavour. And this is important!!!
(IRVING *tries to control himself for a moment. Breathes deeply.*)
Or maybe you wish to let these hooligans determine what can and cannot be presented on our stages? In our books! By our speakers!! Is that what you want?!

CLARK: Of course I don't –.

IRVING: (*Yells*) Take some responsibility!!! (*Short pause.*) This is what I am saying. What I've been asked to say.

ARNOLD: We don't even know who those people were last night.

IRVING: They are vermin!!

MACREADY: Who hate English people.
(*Everyone turns to* MACREADY. *Short pause.*)

IRVING: (*Breathing heavily*) Mr Macready is partially correct. They do hate English people. But that is not where their hate ends. They hate culture. They hate art and books and poems and music and thought!! They hate anything that is civilized!!
(*Beat.*)
We have all seen this side of some of our countrymen, have we not? (*Sighs.*) Could I sit down, please?
(CLARK *gets him a chair, he sits, covers his face.*)
In London you see it so rarely. And in Spain and Italy –

never have I noticed it. But here . . . (*Pause. He suddenly looks up at the others and tries to smile.*) I have been criticized for being – European. My books have . . . (*Stops himself.*) Some things I do not understand any more.
(*Short pause.*)

MACREADY: And –. (*Beat. Looks at the other actors*) Mr Forrest has been spoken to.

IRVING: Mr Forrest, of course, has had nothing to do with any of this, with last night or with anything else. He is a very cultured man. I have borrowed many books from his library.
(*Short pause.*)

MACREADY: He has been spoken to.

IRVING: Mr Forrest has decided on his own to perform only *Metamora* for some time. There'll be no more –. (*Shrugs.*) Not that this had anything to do with last night. But we can thank him for his consideration. (*Short pause.*)
(*Taking a piece of paper out of his pocket*) Now I have here in my hand a letter signed by our leading citizens giving to you their word that should you agree to another performance, you shall be assured of protection. You shall be safe. (*Hands it to an actor.*) Police will be stationed throughout the theatre and outside. (*Beat.*) They mayor has put the militia on notice.

BRIDGES: The militia?!
(*The actors all begin to speak at once:* 'Why do we need the militia?' 'They only bring out the militia if they think –.' 'They're just being safe.' *etc.*)

MACREADY: (*Quietly*) Excuse me.
(*No one hears him.*)
Excuse me. (*He taps* CLARK *on the shoulder.*)

CLARK: Quiet! Quiet!
(*They quieten down.* MACREADY *looks at the actors – one by one.*)

MACREADY: Not that it will affect anyone of you in making a decision. (*Beat.*) But you might like to know that our producers have offered us 75 per cent of the house. (*Beat.*) Fifty to me. Twenty-five to be split by you. (*Beat.*) It's generous. (*Beat.*) But I'm not sure money is the . . . (*Shrugs.*)

The –. (*Beat.*) But it's generous. (*Short pause.*) So think it over. Mr Irving is having food brought up from the dining room. So please stay and eat what you like.

(*Awkward pause. No one knows quite what to do; slowly they begin to mill about and talk quietly with each other.* MRS POPE *goes to* MACREADY. IRVING *is left alone, sitting in the middle of the room. He smiles to others who smile back, though they don't approach him.*)

MRS POPE: (*To* MACREADY) How are you feeling? We've been terribly worried about you.

MACREADY: Thank you. I am much better.

MRS POPE: That was a nasty cut.

MACREADY: It has been seen to.

(*Others line up now – almost like a reception line – in front of* MACREADY *to pay their respects.*)

BRADSHAW: Mr Macready.

MACREADY: Mr Bradshaw. (*Beat.*) Mr Bradshaw, perhaps Banquo and Macbeth should enter together – as it says, I believe, in the text. (*Beat.*) Perhaps Banquo should enter downstage of Macbeth. Even in front of him.

BRADSHAW: (*Playing along with the joke*) Oh Mr Macready, I don't think my character would ever do that.

(MACREADY *smiles;* BRADSHAW *smiles.*)

MACREADY: Still we should rehearse it and see.

WEMYSS: Sir.

MACREADY: And how is your lovely daughter, Mr Wemyss? Does she still want to become an actress?

WEMYSS: She's a thick one.

MACREADY: We never learn.

WEMYSS: No, sir, we don't.

MACREADY: Mrs Pope. Can I count on you to attend rehearsal tomorrow morning?

MRS POPE: The morning? (*Beat.*) If it isn't an inconvenience – the afternoon would be a lot better for me. My sister's staying with me with her two children and she works in the mornings. But maybe I could ask Mrs Seymour, she lives just below – .

MACREADY: (*Smiling*) Come when you can.

MRS POPE: But Mrs Seymour doesn't walk very well. Since she hurt her leg . . . (*She turns and looks at the other actors who are smiling, trying not to laugh.*) What is funny? If it's an inconvenience to anyone. (*They burst out laughing.*) I don't understand why you are laughing.
(*They slowly stop laughing; an angel of silence passes through the room.*)
(*To* WEMYSS) An angel just passed.
IRVING: (*Rather loud*) I've been meaning to have actors to *my* home for years. You're all so much fun. So full of . . . (*Beat.*) Of life.
BRADSHAW: (*To* BRIDGES) I'm glad he said 'life'.
IRVING: I have a story! (*Beat.*) Once when I was in one of our amateur theatricals. You knew of course that I have been many times an amateur actor. (*Smiles, no response. Continues.*) Some of the amateur actors – Mr Cooper was one you'd be interested to know. (*He smiles, but they don't seem to understand who he is talking about.*) Mr Cooper. He's written – . I don't know how many books. (*Beat.*) Mr Cooper? Mr James Fenimore Cooper? (*Beat.*) You must have read . . .
CLARK: I think I have. (*He hasn't.*) Something. I don't remember what. But it was good though.
IRVING: Anyway, in this amateur theatrical, there are soldiers running through a wood. The trees are about so far apart. (*He smiles.*) And one actor runs with his gun like this. (*Horizontal*) And it gets caught on the trees and he flips over and the whole army behind him – all five or six of us – we flip over him! (*He laughs and laughs. No one else does. Short pause.*) Every one of you must have stories like that.
MACREADY: And what about you, Mr Clark? Will we see you tomorrow?
(*Beat.* CLARK *shrugs, then nods.*)
CLARK: I'm an actor.
(*Beat.* MACREADY *suddenly laughs; others turn.*)
MACREADY: (*Laughing*) That's just what *I* said, when they asked me!
(*Finally a servant with a tray brings in the food.*)

65

IRVING: The food!
   (*The actors go to the food and in an instant it is gone.* IRVING
   stands amazed.)
   I guess I should have ordered more.
   (*Blackout.*)

                            SCENE 3

Projection: 11 p.m.

The tavern.
   BOUCICAULT, AGNES *and* FISHER *at one smallish table.* FISHER
is reading Boucicault's play. At a table nearby, TILTON *and* SCOTT,
who has a bandaged hand, sit and drink.
   As the scene begins RYDER *has just entered; he has been stopped at*
Tilton's table to be introduced to SCOTT.

TILTON: Mr Ryder played Macduff, when you – . The other
   night – .
SCOTT: Oh yes. How do you do?
TILTON: He was quite good.
SCOTT: Oh how nice.
RYDER: There wasn't much time to . . . (*Smiles.*) You
   understand.
SCOTT: That's how the theatre often works. If one doesn't like it
   then one gets out.
   (*Turns to* TILTON *and laughs.*)
RYDER: How is the finger? (*Beat.*) I hope . . . Everyone was
   hoping . . .
SCOTT: The finger is gone, Mr – .
   (*Turns to* TILTON.)
TILTON: Ryder.
SCOTT: And at the moment I can't move my hand at all. (*Beat.*)
   They say that will change. Some time.
   (*Beat.*)
RYDER: I heard you were a wonderful Macduff. That you are a – .
   I'm sure I didn't do justice . . . (*Beat.*) No doubt your public
   was profoundly disappointed with me last night.

                              66

SCOTT: My public?
   (*Laughs and pours himself a drink.*)
RYDER: Excuse me, I have friends . . . (*He nods towards
   Boucicault's table.* SCOTT *does not look at him.*)
SCOTT: (*To* TILTON) Who's buying by the way? I don't have any
   money.
   (RYDER *goes to Boucicault's table.*)
TILTON: Don't worry about that.
SCOTT: I wasn't worrying.
RYDER: (*Sitting at Boucicault's table*) Sorry. I dropped by
   backstage. I asked Ned to join us, but – . I don't know. (*They
   nod. Beat.*) Mind if I – ?
BOUCICAULT: No, no, of course not.
   (RYDER *pours himself a drink.*)
RYDER: (*Nodding toward* SCOTT) I took over for him in – . As
   Macduff. He – . There had been an accident with – .
AGNES: We heard about that, didn't we?
BOUCICAULT: The finger?
RYDER: That's right.
   (*Short pause.* BOUCICAULT *watches* FISHER *for a reaction as he
   reads.*)
AGNES: (*Turns to* TILTON) The performance tonight was terribly
   exciting. Thank you. I didn't know this play.
TILTON: Which play are you – ?
AGNES: We were at *Metamora*. The three of us. (*Beat.*) Actually
   we were hoping that the rest of the company . . .
TILTON: I don't think they're coming. Sometimes no one goes
   out. Sometimes it's only me.
SCOTT: But if you're going out – .
TILTON: It's the closest tavern. (*Short pause.*) Some of them have
   to go home. (*Beat.*) Scott here always had to go home. His
   wife made him.
SCOTT: Now she's sick of me. (*Turns to* TILTON) Still she doesn't
   give me any money.
   (*He shakes his head in disgust.*)
TILTON: You saw it tonight? It was good tonight. I liked
   everything I did.
RYDER: Forrest was extraordinary.

67

AGNES: Wasn't he? There was a rawness, like some powerful
    animal – .
RYDER: The nobleness of the character. That's what I was
    taken – .
SCOTT: I play the Indian who betrays him.
RYDER: That's a very interesting role.
SCOTT: (*To* TILTON) Who played him tonight?
TILTON: Jones.
SCOTT: Jones? (*Smiles and shakes his head.*) I knew he wanted to
    play my character.
    (*Short pause.*)
AGNES: Everyone was very good. Thank you. (*She turns back to
    her table. To* RYDER) It is a pity Mr Macready did not feel – .
RYDER: I don't blame him. I wouldn't want to sit in a theatre of
    all places, not after last – .
AGNES: He would have had a good time. He could have forgotten,
    at least for a short while – .
RYDER: I only asked him once, I knew there was no – .
BOUCICAULT: But to see Mr Forrest in a native role. This is what
    he's missed. (*Beat.*) Tonight you could really see his talent. I
    don't think an Englishman could play such an Indian nearly
    so well. (*Beat.*) As an American I think he – . I don't know.
    It is somehow closer to you. Indians, I mean. It must be.
RYDER: I suppose.
BOUCICAULT: It must be how Americans see us with
    Shakespeare. Where we can – . Any of our actors can just off
    to Warwickshire whenever – . Even see the house – . See the
    grave.
AGNES: I'm not sure they feel that – .
BOUCICAULT: They must. (*Beat.*) He was English after all.
TILTON: (*Changing the subject, to the other table*) Shame about Mr
    Macready.
BOUCICAULT: I was there, you know. (*Shakes his head.*)
    Extraordinary. The look on Macready's face. He – I'm sure –
    thought they were going to kill him.
    (*He smiles.*)
RYDER: I don't think it's funny.
BOUCICAULT: Of course it's not funny. I didn't say it was. (*Beat.*)

Anyway, *I* thought he could have kept performing.

AGNES: Dion – .

BOUCICAULT: It wasn't that many people for Christ's sake. But
. . . (*Beat.*) Whatever, it's all part of a day for an actor.
(*Laughs.*) Sometimes they love us, sometimes they – .

SCOTT: I think they should have shot him. That's what I would
have liked to see.

(FISHER *stops reading and looks up.*)

TILTON: Come on, that's – .

SCOTT: I mean it. (*Beat.*) He has no right to be here. People like
him have no right. So he gets what he deserves. This is my
opinion. (*Beat.*) I mean, why the hell did we fight a war?
Why did we fight two wars?! They invade us! We threw
them off! We don't need the goddamn English telling us – .

FISHER: Stop it, Scott.

SCOTT: American actors for America! I don't see what is so wrong
with that?!

RYDER: I doubt if the point of those hooligans was to support
American actors.

SCOTT: What hooligans? Who are you calling hooligans? You
don't even know why they did what they did.

RYDER: And you do?

SCOTT: If they're like me, they're just fed up. You fight war after
war – .

TILTON: When did you fight a war? You didn't fight, Scott.

SCOTT: I wanted to. I was too young. I would have if I had been
older.

FISHER: Tilton is the only one of us who fought . . .

TILTON: I fought and I didn't die. That's all that's worth
remembering.

(*Beat.*)

SCOTT: (*Suddenly stands and points to* RYDER) He took my job!

FISHER: *You* cut off your finger!

SCOTT: I slipped!

FISHER: Blame Jones too then! He's got your role too!

SCOTT: I do blame him! He was a friend. I was nice to him.

FISHER: But he's not English.

SCOTT: He's from Maryland. I've learned in my life never to trust someone from Maryland. I should have listened to myself.

FISHER: So it's people from Maryland, people from England. You're talking nonsense.

SCOTT: Is it nonsense that when we go to their country, they spit in our face?!

TILTON: Are you talking Maryland or England now?

SCOTT: (*Points to* RYDER) Ask him, he knows what I'm talking about!

BOUCICAULT: We have never spat in your – .

TILTON: (*To* SCOTT) When have you ever even been to England?

SCOTT: (*Pointing to* BOUCICAULT *and* RYDER) You make fun of us! (*Turns to* TILTON.) Don't be an idiot, Tilton, you know they do! We don't need them, that's all I want to say. (*Beat.*) Go home! Leave us alone! We don't want you! We don't need you taking our jobs!

RYDER: (*To* AGNES) All this is about is my playing Macduff – .

TILTON: It's his accident. Excuse him.

SCOTT: Don't apologize – .

TILTON: You're grouchy, Scott. (*Beat.*) He's grouchy. (*Beat.*) Ask his wife. Why do you think she let him out? Because he's been so grouchy. (*Tries to laugh. To* SCOTT) If your wife heard you talk like that . . .

SCOTT: Shut up.

FISHER: Don't embarrass yourself!
(*Pause.*)

TILTON: Just a few months ago he was saying how much he wanted to visit England. (*To* SCOTT) Weren't you? (*Beat.*) To visit London. (*Beat.*) It must be very nice.
(*Awkward pause.*)

FISHER: (*Starting a new conversation*) So, what part do you want me to play? I don't understand.

BOUCICAULT: (*Taking his play*) The role is Hamlet. I told you that.

FISHER: But Hamlet – as far as I can tell – has about five lines.

BOUCICAULT: This is true. He comes into Shakespeare's study and tries to help him figure out what he should do about being in love with his neighbour.

FISHER: And he does this in five lines.

BOUCICAULT: The part is Hamlet for Christ's sake. (*Beat. To*

70

AGNES) I don't think I've ever met an actor who didn't want to play Hamlet. (*Turns back to* FISHER.) But then maybe you'd rather play Romeo.

FISHER: How big is Romeo?

BOUCICAULT: Five, six lines. Like Hamlet.

FISHER: Then maybe I could play both.

BOUCICAULT: Play both Hamlet and Romeo?

FISHER: Or does that sound too greedy?

BOUCICAULT: It's an interesting thought but they appear in the same scene. (*Opens the script.*) Here. Romeo arrives in Stratford while Hamlet is still there and tries to find out why Shakespeare isn't writing any more. (*Beat.*) Hamlet of course already knows why, but hasn't told anyone.

RYDER: (*Holding up a pitcher of beer, to* SCOTT *and* TILTON) We have some beer.

(TILTON *turns to Scott.*)

SCOTT: No, thank you.

(*Short pause.*)

FISHER: Who played Hamlet in the London production?

BOUCICAULT: What was his name? (*Turns to* AGNES.) A very good actor, wasn't he? The next Kean, everyone was saying. He found a lot to do with the part. (*Beat.*) There's a lot there.

FISHER: And he just played Hamlet? Not Timon of Athens too or anything else?

BOUCICAULT: Timon isn't in the play. (*Beat.*) He didn't seem to fit. (*Beat.*) We're just talking about a reading. There's no pay, of course. There's usually not for a reading, I understand. (*Beat.*) But of course then when the play is produced – . Hackett has practically guaranteed . . .

FISHER: What are the dates? Hackett's dates?

BOUCICAULT: (*Shrugs*) Some time in November, I think. (*To* AGNES) November?

FISHER: That might be a problem. Early November or late?

BOUCICAULT: Which is better?

FISHER: I might be doing a play in Philadelphia in early November. (*Beat.*) Nothing's set. But they want me. I know they want me. Who's going to play Shakespeare? That seems to be the part?

71

BOUCICAULT: We don't have a Shakespeare as yet.

FISHER: Am I too young? Is that what you think? How old is
Shakespeare anyway? (BOUCICAULT *shrugs*.) I hate it when
people say you're too young, you're too old, you're too
whatever. To me that's just ridiculous! What if I said I was
only interested in playing Shakespeare in your play?

BOUCICAULT: You don't want to play Hamlet?

FISHER: I'm not saying that. I'm just asking – .

BOUCICAULT: I can't offer you Shakespeare. (*Turns to* AGNES.)
We can't.

FISHER: I thought you said you don't have a – .

BOUCICAULT: We don't. But someone else is reading the part.
(*To* AGNES) Isn't he? I can't offer you – . Not while someone
is reading – . You understand, I'm sure.

FISHER: That's fair. (*Beat*.) You really say this was a big success?

BOUCICAULT: It was in – . In London.

FISHER: It seems sort of stupid to me.

BOUCICAULT: Stupid?

FISHER: A waste. I mean you bring on Hamlet for one, maybe
two little scenes. I think you're missing something terrific
here. Let me look at it again.

(FISHER *takes the script back.* BOUCICAULT *turns to* AGNES
*and nearly rolls his eyes – all this just to cast a small role in a
reading.*)
Hackett?

BOUCICAULT: That's right.

FISHER: I like Hackett. I've worked with him a lot. (*Beat*.)
Though I never thought he'd hire me to play Hamlet.
(*He smiles, pleased with his good fortune.* FORREST *enters.*)

RYDER: There he is! It's Ned.

AGNES: (*To* BOUCICAULT) He came.

FORREST: Forgive me, I forgot where John said you were going to
go.

BOUCICAULT: Sit down, sit down. Here's a glass.
(FORREST *sits;* BOUCICAULT *pours him a glass.*)

AGNES: I can't tell you how much we loved the performance – .

SCOTT: (*Calls out*) Ned! (FORREST *turns.*) Ned?
(*He suddenly gets up.*)

FORREST: Mr Scott, what a surprise! You weren't in the audience tonight – .

SCOTT: No, no. I wasn't.

TILTON: I dragged him out of the house – .

SCOTT: My wife threw me out – . (*Beat.*) For the night.

TILTON: He'd been driving her – .

FORREST: How's the finger?

SCOTT: I'm getting better. They say in a few days, I'll . . .

FORREST: That's good to hear. (*Beat.*) You'd be proud of young Jones. He's doing his best.

SCOTT: Good. *That's* very good to hear. (*Beat.*) They really say that in a few days – .

FORREST: Let me buy you a drink.

SCOTT: No, no, please, it's I who should – .

FORREST: What are you drinking? Here. (*Puts money on the table.*) You're looking great.

(*He smiles and goes back to his table. Short pause.*)

BOUCICAULT: I enjoyed tonight a great deal.

(FORREST *nods.*)

It made me think perhaps I should try my hand at an American theme. (*Turns to* RYDER.) Maybe an Indian play as well.

AGNES: It seemed very authentic.

(FORREST *turns and looks at* FISHER, *who looks up.*)

FISHER: Mr Boucicault's play. He wants me to play Hamlet.

BOUCICAULT: (*Quickly*) In the reading. This Saturday. You'll be there, I hope.

FISHER: I don't know yet if I'm available for the full production.

BOUCICAULT: (*To* FORREST) So we'll have to hold our breath for a while.

(*Short pause.*)

FORREST: (*Distracted, points to a glass*) Is this mine?

AGNES: That one there. Yes.

(FORREST *drinks.*)

FORREST: The house was full tonight I gather. It felt that way.

BOUCICAULT: Packed.

AGNES: Thank you for the seats.

RYDER: The couple next to us was sobbing at the end.

73

(*Beat.*)

AGNES: I was sobbing at the end.

(*Beat.*)

BOUCICAULT: If I *were* to attempt an Indian play, Mr Forrest, I don't imagine you'd be interested in seeing – .

FORREST: (*Not listening*) Sometimes you can feel an audience giving back as much as you are trying to give them. (*Beat.*) It felt like that. You were a good audience.

BOUCICAULT: I know exactly what you mean.

FORREST: And sometimes – . (*Turns to* RYDER.) How is Mr Macready? I meant to write him today.

RYDER: He's – . In shock? (*Shrugs.*) How should he be?

BOUCICAULT: I was there, you know. We were. It was unbelievable.

FORREST: (*To* RYDER) What about his wounds? I heard – . He was cut?

BOUCICAULT: There was blood all over the stage. When he walked off, Macready's face was covered. You couldn't see his – .

RYDER: It was a cut. On his forehead. (*Turns to* BOUCICAULT.) It looked worse than it was.

(*Short pause.*)

FORREST: (*Without looking at anyone*) I've heard someone – . Someone was saying – I forget who it was – they were saying that people think I'm somehow . . . (*Beat.*) That I bear a responsibility.

BOUCICAULT: For last night?

FORREST: This is what I've heard.

FISHER: People are nervous, all kinds of things are being said.

RYDER: I have heard this as well, Mr Forrest. You try to tell people that – .

AGNES: No one can – .

FORREST: As if attacking Macready's *Macbeth* was somehow praising mine. This is thinking I do not grasp myself. (*Smiles.*) It's ridiculous. It's unfair. If they knew – . If only someone had come to me and said there could be trouble. I now understand there were threats made days ago.

RYDER: Mr Forrest – .

FORREST: Let me finish. Where was Mr Macready? Why did he

not confide in me? We had dinner only the other day. He said nothing, isn't that right, Mr Ryder? You were there.

RYDER: That's correct.

FORREST: Just the other day, we had dinner. My wife and I did. (*Beat. Sighs.*) As if I don't have enough to worry about. (*Beat.*) We don't know who these thugs were, do we? Or even what they wanted. (*Shakes his head.*) It seems so unnecessary. (*Beat.*) How many were there? I've heard at least ten different accounts.

BOUCICAULT: They were in the balcony. Most of them were in the balcony, weren't they?

FORREST: I've even heard . . . (*Beat.*) I'm sure this is not true. You were there. I'm sure he did the right thing. (*Beat.*) But someone was saying – . Who was it? (*Shrugs.*) They were saying that if Macready had only stayed on the stage and shouted back at them.

AGNES: He tried this. (*Turns to* BOUCICAULT.) Have you – .

FORREST: Oh. Then he tried.

BOUCICAULT: Not for that long though.

FORREST: Really? (*Beat.*) I mean we've all had audiences that – . I don't know. Can't be pleased, I suppose. Nothing will please them. (*Beat.*) We get such audiences here. Maybe not in England, but – .

BOUCICAULT: You get them in England. You really get them in Scotland.

AGNES: Scotland can be bad, this is true.

FORREST: Then you know what I'm talking about. How sometimes one needs to fight back. To assert oneself. You let a crowd have their way . . . (*Shrugs.*) If you don't lead . . . (*Beat.*) I'm sure it's not true, but it is possible that Mr Macready – for whatever reason – was simply unable to lead. Unable to do his job. (*Beat.*) And so – he ran away.

RYDER: I don't think that's fair.

FORREST: Is it fair to blame me?
   (*Short pause.*)

RYDER: No. That isn't fair either.

FORREST: Because some unhappy people decide to rip up some seats while shouting out my name?

75

RYDER: They shouted your name? That I hadn't heard. (*To* BOUCICAULT) Did you – ?

BOUCICAULT: They did. That's true.

FORREST: I'm an actor. What can I do? (*Beat.*) People sit in their seats and dream about you, until what they dream isn't you. (*Beat.*) What people shout . . . (*Shrugs.*) I have enough things . . . (*Short pause.*) He should have just yelled them down. Had the guts to yell them down. And then all of this . . .

(MACREADY *enters with* CLARK *and* BRADSHAW.)

MACREADY: Mr Forrest.

(FORREST *turns and stands.*)

FORREST: You don't look any worse for wear. Please, won't you – .

MACREADY: We just took a table in the next room. I heard you were here and . . . (*Beat.*) I want to thank you for changing to *Metamora*.

(FORREST *nods.*)

It will help to – . This so-called rivalry.

FORREST: What rivalry? (*Beat.*) I heard that in some quarters we are both being blamed for what happened last night.

MACREADY: I had not heard that we both were being blamed.

RYDER: Mr Forrest was just saying that they were shouting out his name.

MACREADY: I remember hearing it very distinctly.

FORREST: It will all calm down.

MACREADY: Of course it will. (*Beat.*) It has nothing to do with us, does it?

FORREST: No. Nothing.

(*Beat.*)

MACREADY: (*Suddenly turns to* RYDER) Where have you been, John? I expected to see you this evening.

RYDER: I went to Mr Forrest's *Metamora*. I told you I was going. I asked you to go.

MACREADY: Did you? (*Beat.*) I suppose it is all very – original. My loss, no doubt. Get us some liquor, will you? Different kinds. You choose. (*Turns to go, stops, goes back.*) Oh. I forgot. You need my money, don't you? (*Puts money on the table.*) Don't be too long.

76

(*He and* CLARK *and* BRADSHAW – *who have stayed at some distance – now leave. Pause.*)

RYDER: I better . . . (*He stands.*) Perhaps, first I'll finish my wine. (*He sits.*) I just have a sip left. (*Drinks it.*)

FORREST: Let me fill up your glass.

(*After some hesitation,* RYDER *hands him his glass.* FORREST *pours him another drink.*)

On tour, a few years ago, in a small southern town, I happened to cast as my Ophelia, the daughter of a preacher. (*Beat.*) I had not known this. And the true extent of his rage had been kept from me. (*Beat.*) But as I made my first entrance, I heard the clicks of many revolvers being cocked. (*Beat.*) You know, it never occurred to me to leave that stage.

(*Pause, then:*
Blackout.)

SCENE 4

Projection: 2 a.m.

A small attic apartment.

FORREST *and* RYDER *come up the stairs (up through a trap); they carry lanterns.*

FORREST: I'm surprised you're even interested. Watch your step.

RYDER: I'm interested in talking about anything. And everything.

FORREST: (*Holding up the lantern and looking around the room*) I told you it was small. But it is convenient. Put it over there. (RYDER *sets down his lantern.*) Sit down, sit down. (*Beat.*) One block from the theatre. (*He lights another lantern.*) It is a place to get away.

RYDER: I'm sure – .

FORREST: Sit down, please, Mr Ryder. And when they throw you out of the tavern, it is a place to get a drink. Let me get you that drink. (*Goes to a cabinet and takes out a bottle, glasses, etc.*

77

Pause.) It's cold tonight. Cold for May. (*Beat.*) Feels like it's going to rain. But that I am sure is something you are used to.

RYDER: Rain? (*Smiles.*) I don't miss it.

FORREST: Do you miss anything? (*Beat.*) Won't you miss – ?

RYDER: I haven't agreed to anything, Mr – . Ned. I thought we were just . . . (*Beat.*) I'd probably be interested in a season. (*Beat.*) A four- or five-month season. Depending on where it is. Where are you going. There's much more of this country I'd like to see. I'm not homesick yet. (*Looks at him.*) I admired your performance tonight enormously.
(*Door opens and* MISS BASS *enters, a blanket around her shoulders. Underneath she is naked, having just been woken up.*)

MISS BASS: What time is it – ? (*Sees* RYDER.) Oh, I'll . . . I didn't know you'd . . .

FORREST: Have a drink with us, Jane. You know John, of course.

MISS BASS: Yes, of course. Let me get some clothes on.
(*She goes. Pause.*)

FORREST: She lives here. (*Beat.*) She looks after it for me. (*Beat.*) I'm pleased you enjoyed *Metamora* tonight. I paid for that play, you know. Had a contest. The best play on an American topic. (*Beat.*) That came in. It was a mess. Wrote three-quarters of it myself. (*Beat.*) Fits like a glove now. Could play some of it in my sleep. And they can't get enough of it. Anywhere I go. (*Beat.*) You'll see yourself. (*Beat.*) I don't need anyone for *Metamora*.

RYDER: I wasn't suggesting – . That's not why I – .

FORREST: I need a Buckingham. (*Beat.*) A Mercutio. An Edgar, son of Gloucester. As well as Macduff of course.

RYDER: That's very generous.

FORREST: Between you and me . . . We can talk about Iago another time.

RYDER: I've played Iago.

FORREST: That's good to know. (*Short pause.*) In my production he's very subtle. The man who plays him now is very good.

RYDER: I'll come and see – .

FORREST: We do New Orleans, St Louis, Cincinnati, then to Baltimore and Philadelphia. Then back here for a month for

78

Hackett. (*Beat.*) This is November.

RYDER: I thought Boucicault's play was to be done by Hackett in – .

FORREST: The problem of course is can I afford you. (*Beat.*) You are probably very expensive.

RYDER: You know what you paid for one Macduff.

FORREST: You are very expensive.

(MISS BASS *enters, having quickly dressed.*)

(*Getting up*) Let me get you a – .

MISS BASS: I can get a drink myself.

(FORREST *sits back down. Short pause.*)

RYDER: I should probably be – .

(*He starts to stand.*)

FORREST: Don't be silly. Sit down. We don't have that many guests, do we?

(*He sits. Short pause.*)

MISS BASS: I'm sorry I couldn't join you at the tavern tonight. I was exhausted. (*Beat.*) Did I miss anything?

FORREST: Did you miss – ? Did she, John?

RYDER: I . . .

(*He shrugs. He has been fiddling with a manuscript that is in front of him.*)

FORREST: Boucicault's play. Take a look if you want. (*Beat.*) I'm supposed to be reading it. (*Beat.*) He asked me to – . (*Turns to* MISS BASS.) I've read most of it. I've read some of it. He says Macready's interested if you can believe that.

RYDER: I doubt if – . (*Beat.*) I don't know.

MISS BASS: I've tried to read it tonight.

(*She rolls her eyes and laughs. Short pause.*)

FORREST: John loved *Metamora*.

MISS BASS: Ned wrote most of that.

(*Pause.*)

RYDER: It's a lovely apartment. (*To* MISS BASS) It's yours?

(*She turns to* FORREST, *then back.*)

MISS BASS: Yeah. (*Beat.*) It's mine.

RYDER: It's very convenient.

MISS BASS: Isn't it?

FORREST: John has asked to join us for a season.

79

RYDER: I haven't actually – . (*Stops himself, smiles.*) If Ned can
find a place for me.
(*Short pause.*)
(*Suddenly stands.*) Really, it is late. I must go. (*No one gets
up.*) Thank you for the drink.
FORREST: (*Gesturing that he could stand*) Let me.
RYDER: I think I can let myself out. (*He takes the lantern.*) Miss
Bass. (*Beat.*) Ned.
(*He goes. Long pause.*)
MISS BASS: (*Finally*) Do you want to go to bed?
(*He doesn't respond.*)
It was nice having company. It was nice to – . Entertain.
This way. (*Beat.*) He's a nice man. Why he wants to work in
America when – .
FORREST: He liked my performance. He wants to work with me.
MISS BASS: I didn't mean . . . (*Beat.*) He must have many
reasons. Maybe things in England weren't working out so
. . . I don't know, Ned. I'm sorry I brought it up.
(*He sips his drink. Short pause.*)
I ran into our landlord this morning. (*Beat.*) The rent's due.
(*Beat.*) I know I reminded you already, but – . I didn't know
if you'd forgotten. (*Beat.*) Sometimes you do forget. (*She
laughs. He doesn't seem to hear her.*) Ned? (*Beat.*) My – . (*She
opens her mouth.*) I broke a tooth.
(*He looks at her.*)
I'm sorry to bring it up now. I know you're tired but – .
(*Beat.*) This is the only chance we seem to have, so . . .
(*He takes out some money and sets it down.*)
I don't like to beg.
FORREST: You're not begging.
(*Short pause.*)
MISS BASS: My mother wrote. She's finally coming to visit. I
don't believe it, I've asked her a hundred times. (*Beat.*) I
guess she finally accepts my being an actress. (*She laughs to
herself.*) She wants to stay here. She thinks it's – . Mine.
(*Beat.*) She'll stay for three weeks.
(*Short pause.* FORREST *just sits there.*)
Do you mind? (*Beat.*) Do you mind?

80

(Short pause.
Blackout.)

SCENE 5

Projection: Later that night.

Macready's rooms, New York Hotel.
    MACREADY *asleep, drunk, in a chair.* RYDER *sits in another chair, reading Boucicault's manuscript. Pause. Suddenly* MACREADY *screams – he's having a nightmare.*

RYDER: It's all right. Calm down. It's me. It's me.
    (MACREADY *opens his eyes, he breathes heavily; looks around him.*)
    You had a dream.
    (*Pause. Heavy breathing; rubs his eyes.*)
MACREADY: How long have I – . When did you . . . ?
RYDER: You asked me in, remember? We were talking. You were telling me about the meeting. (*Beat.*) With Irving. (*Beat.*) You fell asleep.
MACREADY: What time is it?
RYDER: Nearly half past four.
MACREADY: I can't sleep in my bed.
RYDER: That's what you'd been saying . . . That's why – .
    (*Gestures 'I am here'.*) Let me get you a drink. It helped before.
MACREADY: I'm going to smell for days. (*Smiles.*) My spit will intoxicate at least the first three rows. (*Wider smile.* RYDER *brings him a drink. He sips.*) It was an actor's dream, John.
RYDER: Not surprising.
MACREADY: The actor's dream. (*Beat.*) Do cobblers and coat-makers have their dreams? One wonders. Though mine was an interesting variation. It wasn't that I could not remember my lines or what part I was playing or which play I was in, rather – it was the reverse. (*Beat.*) In my dream, I was speaking all the parts. One second I was – . whatever. I can't

81

remember. Then the next, I was speaking back to me. Then entering to tell me something. Then telling me to leave so I could be alone and have my soliloquy. (*Beat.*) Rather exhausting this was. And rather unnerving to the other actors whose parts I was obviously usurping. Thus one by one they – my fellow actors – retreated from the stage and allowed me to be alone with various other me's. (*Beat.*) One or two left quite angrily too. This I could not understand. After all I was much better than they could ever hope to be. They should have appreciated this.

(*Short pause.*)

When it came time for Macduff to kill Macbeth – so obviously this was *Macbeth* – I found myself in a quandary, of course. (*Laughs to himself.*) The audience was cheering. They screamed. Were they praising my performing? Were they after my death? I did not understand the effect I was having. (*Beat.*) And then – as the script calls for it – I killed myself, or rather my Macduff killed my Macbeth. And the pain, it was horrific.

(*Short pause. Looks at* RYDER.)

I knew every part and was good. (*Laughs. Beat.*) I shall be afraid now to go to sleep again. The sun should be up when?

(RYDER *shrugs.*)

What time did you come here?

RYDER: It was a little after two.

MACREADY: And I was up then?

RYDER: I think you had been asleep, but . . .

(*Short pause.*)

MACREADY: (*Suddenly starts*) Had I written to my wife?! I always write to my wife!

RYDER: Yes. you had. It's . . .

(*He nods to the table. Short pause.*)

MACREADY: (*Suddenly starts again*) And when you came, there were crowds in the streets. Angry crowds!

RYDER: No. (*Beat.*) The streets were . . . A few carts. A few people. (*Beat.*) That must have been another dream.

(MACREADY *notices the manuscript in* RYDER's *hands.*)

Boucicault's play. I see he gave you a copy. (*Beat.*) Did you read it?

MACREADY: I looked at it. (*Beat.*) Forrest is interested. That's
what one hears.
RYDER: I wouldn't know. I don't – . (*Beat.*) Maybe.
(*Pause.*)
MACREADY: They say I will be safe. Besides the police they may
even circle the entire theatre with soldiers. Nothing can
happen. (*Beat.*) Soldiers. (*Beat.*) What a country. And now
you want to stay here. This is what you were telling me,
wasn't it? (*Beat.*) See, I was awake.
RYDER: I didn't think – .
MACREADY: I was even listening.
(*Beat.*)
RYDER: Then you know, and that is that.
MACREADY: Is it? (*Beat.*) I paid your way here *and* back, Mr
Ryder.
RYDER: I have done everything you've asked.
MACREADY: You were brought here to work for me, not for Mr
Forrest!
RYDER: I shall make sure you are safely on a ship and very
comfortable. That's where my responsibility ends!
(*Pause.*)
MACREADY: (*To himself*) Alone on the stage. The actors are
deserting me. Dreams and life. Life and dreams. How can
you stomach such a country where soldiers stand around
theatres?! (*Beat.*) When audiences – . But of course you
didn't see this. You were busy playing for Mr Forrest.
RYDER: You agreed that I could.
MACREADY: How could I say no? (*Beat.*) This does not mean I
approved, John. I had hoped you'd have recognized your
own responsibility. Your own duty. But . . . (*Beat.*) This is
how one learns about one's friends. (*Short pause.*) I will never
employ you again. (*Beat.*) Never.
(*Pause.* RYDER *says nothing.*)
I may change my mind, but that is how I feel at this time,
John. (*Beat.*) I'm planning a season at the Drury Lane.
Nothing has been cast. Except the leads, of course. We can
talk about anything you wish. (*Beat.*) We can talk now.
RYDER: I will be back in a few months. It's only for a few months.

MACREADY: Oh. You didn't say that. (*Beat.*) Then we will talk in those few months. (*Beat.*) How many is a 'few'?
RYDER: Three.
(*Short pause.*)
MACREADY: In two months, I begin to cast.
(*Pause.*)
Forrest has parts for you?
RYDER: If he didn't, he wouldn't be asking – .
MACREADY: Make him give you excellent parts, John! In America you deserve excellent parts, remember that.
RYDER: I saw his *Metamora* tonight.
MACREADY: I have seen this performance. (*Beat.*) Years ago. Seven years or so ago. (*Beat.*) Somewhere. He has power. In this role.
RYDER: Absolutely. When he kills his wife – .
MACREADY: Ah. Yes. True. (*Beat.*) And that must have been quite heartfelt tonight.
(RYDER *looks at* MACREADY.)
His wife has left him, you know.
RYDER: I didn't know. When – ?
MACREADY: Just today. Everyone was telling me. Who told me? After the meeting, someone was saying . . . (*Beat.*) She's staying with a friend. (*Beat.*) Just left him a note.
(*Pause.*)
Metamora is a very good role for him. I would never attempt it myself. (*Beat.*) Audiences love it. (*Shakes his head.*) He's made a fortune from it. (*Beat.*) I understand he's building a castle of some sort just up the Hudson. All from the money he's made from . . . (*Beat.*) Lucky him. (*Beat.*) Every actor is staying. I don't have to replace anyone. I take my hat off to all of them. Not one is deserting. (*Beat. To himself*) Actors. By and large we are good and decent people. (*Beat.*) So they left the stage and there I am trying to kill myself! (*Laughs.*) I can see myself as Macduff. I'd be a very good Macduff. If the part were larger. Mmmmmmmmm. (*Smiles to himself.*) Mmmmmmmmm. I'm waking up. (*Beat.*) Let's wait for the sun to rise. Which, like stage light, will keep us out of the dark.

(*He takes a sip of the drink. Short pause.*
Blackout.)

SCENE 6

Projection: 10 May 1849. 8.30 p.m.

The stage of the Broadway Theatre. The end of the second act of
Metamora.
   The council chamber. ERRINGTON (Blakeley), METAMORA
(Forrest), *and* SOLDIERS.
ERRINGTON: Approach!
   (GOODENOUGH [Miss Burton] *returns with the traitor*
   ANRAWANDAH [Jones].)
METAMORA: Anrawandah!
ERRINGTON: Behold, deceitful man, thy deeds are known.
METAMORA: Let me see his eye. Art thou he whom I snatched
   from the war club of the Mohigan, when thou hadst sung thy
   death song, and the lips of the foe were thirsty for thy blood?
   Has Metamora cherished thee in his wigwam and hast thou
   put a knife into the white man's hand to slay him! The foul
   spirit hath entered thee, and the pure blood of the
   Wampanoag has left they veins. Thy heart is a lie, and thine
   eye cannot rest upon the face of truth, when like the great
   light it shines on thee in unclouded glory. Elders, can he
   speak to you the words of truth, when he is false to his
   brother, his country and his god?
ERRINGTON: He was thy trusty agent, Metamora, and
   conscience-smote revealed thy wickedness.
METAMORA: You believe his words?
ERRINGTON: We do, and will reward his honesty.
METAMORA: Wampanoag! No, I will not call thee so. Red man,
   say unto these people they have bought thy tongue, and thou
   hast uttered a lie!
ERRINGTON: He does not answer.
METAMORA: I am Metamora, thy father and thy king.
ERRINGTON: Metamora o'erawes him – send the witness home.

METAMORA: I will do that! Slave of the white man, go follow
Sasamond.
(METAMORA *stabs* ANRAWANDAH; *general movement.*)
ERRINGTON: Seize and bind him.
(SOLDIERS *make a forward movement.*)
METAMORA: Come! My knife has drunk the blood of the false
one, yet it is not satisfied! White man, beware! The mighty
spirits – .
(FORREST *suddenly stops. Long pause, during which the other
actors do not know what is going on – they are concerned that
FORREST has dried, but try to stay in character. FORREST shows
no panic or concern, it is as if his mind has drifted off. Finally an
actor hits the butt of his gun on the stage and FORREST comes to
and continues*) From the east to the west, in the north and in
the south shall cry of vengeance burst, till the lands you have
stolen groan under your feet no more!
ERRINGTON: Secure him!
METAMORA: Thus do I smite your nation and defy your power.
ERRINGTON: Fire on him.
(METAMORA *hurls a hatchet into the stage and runs out.*
SOLDIERS *fire after him. Drums. Trumpets. Tableau.
Blackout.*)

SCENE 7

Projection: 8.45 p.m.

*The wings of the Astor Place Opera House. The stage of the Opera
House is unseen, just off stage. Macready's* Macbeth *is in progress.
Numerous actors in costume wait and watch. One hears from 'the
stage',* Act II. iii, *beginning with:*

MACBETH: . . . there, the murderers,
Steeped in the colours of their trade, their daggers
Unmannerly breeched with gore. Who could refrain
That had a heart to love, and in that heart
Courage to make's love known?

LADY MACBETH: Help me hence, ho!
MACDUFF: Look to the Lady.
    (*Scene continues 'on stage'*; LADY MACBETH [Mrs Pope] *is
    carried from the stage. As she enters the wings:*)
BRIDGES: How is it?
MRS POPE: A couple of people in the balcony. A couple boos
    nothing else.
    (*She stands on her own, rubs her face and sighs. Actors look at
    each other, when they catch someone's eye, they smile. Sense of
    great tension in the air. On stage is continuing:*)
MACDUFF: And so do I.
ALL: So all.
MACBETH: Lets's briefly put on manly readiness
        And meet i' th' hall together.
ALL: Well contented.
    (MACBETH [Macready], MACDUFF [Clark], BANQUO
    [Bradshaw] *enter from the stage. Scene between* MALCOLM *and*
    DONALBAIN *continues off.*)
MACREADY: (*Entering*) I've played to better houses.
BRADSHAW: They're nervous.
MACREADY: The soldiers still outside?
BRIDGES: There seem to be even more.
MACREADY: Don't complain.
    (MALCOLM [Arnold] *and* DONALBAIN [Sefton] *enter from the
    stage and* BRIDGES [Ross] *and* WEMYSS [Old Man] *leave the
    wings and enter on to the stage for* Act II. iv – *a heavily cut
    version.*)
SEFTON: (*To* MACREADY, *as a joke*) As soon as you get off they
    settle down and listen.
    (*He smiles. Suddenly, from above, the sound of a window being
    smashed by a rock. Everyone stops. One gets the impression that
    the scene on stage and the audience stopped and gasped as one.
    No one comments, the scene on stage continues.*)
MRS POPE: (*To no one in particular*) They're putting in a new
    sewer across the street. Did you notice? (*Beat.*) They've got
    stones piled all over the place.
ARNOLD: I guess some boy couldn't resist.
MRS POPE: That's just what I was thinking.

(CLARK [Macduff] *leaves the wings and joins the scene on stage. From the stage:*)

ROSS: How goes the world, sir, now?

MACDUFF: Why, see you not?

ROSS: Is't known who did this more than bloody deed?

    (*Etc. The scene continues.*)

MACREADY: (*To* MRS POPE) How's your sister?

MRS POPE: Who?

MACREADY: Didn't the other day you say something about your sister visiting?

MRS POPE: Did I? (*Beat.*) She's good. Very good.

    (BRADSHAW [Banquo] *leaves the wings for the stage as* CLARK [Macduff], WEMYSS [Old Man], *and* BRIDGES [Ross] *come into the wings.*)

CLARK: (*Entering*) What is it about that audience? There's something – .

MACREADY: As someone was saying – they're nervous.

CLARK: There's something else. I can't put my finger on it.

MACREADY: (*To* MRS POPE) We're on.

CLARK: Wait a minute! I got it. They're all men! The audience! There aren't any women!

MACREADY: We're on!

    (MACREADY [Macbeth] *and* MRS POPE [Lady Macbeth] *enter the stage, followed by* BRIDGES [Ross] *and others. Trumpet fanfare. From the stage:*)

MACBETH: Here's our chief guest.

LADY MACBETH: If he had been forgotten,

    It had been as a gap in our great feast,

    And all-thing unbecoming.

MACBETH: To-night we hold a solemn supper – .

    (MACREADY *has stopped himself. A stony silence from the audience, then a gasp and screams.*)

CLARK: (*Having run to the edge of the wings*) Someone's tried to jump – . From the balcony. Police are trying to – .

    (*Another broken window. Those in the wings turn.*

    CHIPPINDALE *enters from the dressing-rooms.*)

CHIPPINDALE: They're bolting the doors. They are bolting the doors! We're being locked in!

88

CLARK: (*Looking towards the stage*) They caught the man. The
　　 police have him.
　　 (*A sudden cheer from the audience.* CLARK *and the others sigh.*
　　 The play continues for a moment.)
MACBETH: To-night we hold a solemn supper, sir,
　　 And I'll request your presence.
BANQUO:　　　　　　　　　　　　 Let your Highness
　　 Command upon me, to the which my duties
　　 Are with a most indissoluble tie
　　 For ever knit.
　　 (*Suddenly a number of windows are broken, large rocks crash against
　　 the doors of the theatre. Play continues but hardly audible.*)
CHIPPINDALE: Jesus Christ.
　　 (*Then there is a single gunshot from outside the theatre.*)
CLARK: What was that?
SEFTON: I heard it.
CLARK: Who's firing?
　　 (BRIDGES [Ross] *hurries in from the stage.*)
BRIDGES: What was that? We heard a gunshot.
CLARK: It was from – .
　　 (*Suddenly tens of gunshots ring out from outside as well as cries of
　　 people being seriously hurt. Everyone – including the audience –
　　 is still and listening. The the full-fledged sounds of riot from
　　 outside; sense of the theatre itself under siege.*)
BRIDGES: They're storming the doors. They want to kill us.
　　 (*Panic from the house and the stage;* MACREADY *and the other
　　 actors hurry into the wings.*)
MACREADY: What's going on? Where are the police? Why aren't
　　 the police back here?!
MRS POPE: (*Entering*) They're setting fires in the balcony.
BRADSHAW: Open the doors and get the soldiers in here.
　　 (*Panic. No one knows where to go. The battles being waged in
　　 the house get closer;* ARNOLD *appears from above and throws
　　 down a rope-ladder.*)
ARNOLD: (*Throwing the ladder*) Up here! Climb up! They're
　　 coming on the stage!
　　 (MRS POPE *screams and begins to sob uncontrollably.*)
MACREADY: (*Pulling out his sword*) Fight them off! Fight!

89

(*Banging on the doors continues.* BRIDGES *begins to climb up the ladder.*)

WEMYSS: The doors are breaking in.

BRADSHAW: (*Grabbing others*) Quick through the house. Come on. Through the house. Take off your costumes!

(*Actors start ripping off their costumes. One starts to head towards the stage.*)

Not across the stage! That way! That way! There's a door! (*Grabbing an actor who is taking off his costume*) There's no time! Go! Run!

(*Actors run off.* RYDER *appears from the stage after having obviously battled his way there. He sees* MACREADY.)

RYDER: Mr Macready!

MACREADY: (*Dazed*) Stand back! Stand back! Or die!!!

RYDER: It's John. (*Beat.*) John Ryder. (*Beat.*) It's me.

(MACREADY *finally lets* RYDER *near him.* RYDER *puts a coat over his shoulders.*)

BRADSHAW: Hurry!

(*They all go off. The riot continues off.*
Blackout.)

SCENE 8

Projection: 11.30 p.m.

Forrest's dressing-room; the Broadway Theatre. FORREST, *half-changed out of his costume for* Metamora, *and* RYDER *and* MACREADY, *both dishevelled and out of breath.*

Outside, in the distance, the occasional gunshot and whoops from a roving mob.

RYDER: There were some rocks thrown. Some boys, they – . At first the soldiers fired into the air. But then one or two . . . (*Beat.*) I suppose . . . (*Short pause.*) I figured the last place anyone would think of looking for – .

(*Looks at* MACREADY, *who is very upset, trying desperately to get his breath.*)

90

I need to find some horses. I need to contact friends. My
guess is that they would kill him, it's a riot. No one's in
control. (*Beat.*) The soldiers are running through the streets
firing. The police refused to leave the theatre. (*Laughs to
himself.*) We left with the audience. We just got out and ran.
(*Beat.*) Inside, I don't think there's . . . By now. The seats
were being ripped apart. Someone set a fire under the
balcony. (*Beat.*) From the parquette. (*Beat.*) They just
suddenly were crawling over the seats, over people in the
audience – from the parquette. How they got there . . . It
could all be on fire now.
(*Short pause.*)
FORREST: Are people hurt? Someone must have been hurt.
(RYDER *looks to* MACREADY, *who doesn't answer, then turns
back.*)
RYDER: We saw ourselves – . What? (*Covers his eyes for a moment.*)
People are dead.
FORREST: I don't believe this.
RYDER: Who knows how many. Five, ten, at least. (*To*
MACREADY) Right? (*Beat.*) And a lot wounded. Seriously
wounded. Twenty, thirty, fifty? I don't know.
(*Pause.*)
FORREST: (*Suddenly turns to* MACREADY) You goaded them! Why
did you perform?!
RYDER: That's not fair.
(*Short pause.*)
MACREADY: (*Quietly*) I didn't *goad* anyone. Could I get a drink,
please? The opposite is true.
(FORREST *doesn't move.*)
FORREST: Ten people dead, Mr Macready!
RYDER: I don't know for sure how – .
MACREADY: Could I get a drink, please?!
(RYDER *looks at* FORREST, *then goes to a cabinet and pours the
drink.*)
FORREST: You should not have played.
MACREADY: They begged me. Irving promised me it'd be – . He
had a petition. Everyone said – . (*Beat.*) I wasn't to worry. I
wasn't to . . .

(MACREADY *starts to sob. Short pause.* RYDER *hands*
MACREADY *the drink*.)

FORREST: (*To* RYDER) People killed for what?

MACREADY: (*Suddenly turns*) They were shouting your name again!
(FORREST *turns to* RYDER, *who nods*.)
'Kill Macready! Three Cheers for Ned Forrest!'

FORREST: Why would they do that? That doesn't make sense.

MACREADY: 'Ned Forrest – an American!'

FORREST: I have made it very clear that I – .

MACREADY: I didn't want this! (*Beat*.) After the other night, I . . .

FORREST: When you should have shouted them down. That's your
mistake. You should have had the guts to shout them down!
All of this could have been – !

RYDER: You don't know what you're talking about.
(*Pause*.)

MACREADY: I was told – if I didn't perform – I'd be hurting
American . . . American what? They made it sound like I had
to . . .

FORREST: For 75 per cent of the house! I heard about this!

MACREADY: That had nothing to do with – . (*Beat*.) Money has
nothing to do with this. (*Beat. Attacking*) 'Three cheers for
Ned Forrest. Hurray for Forrest!' As they try to burn down a
theatre!

FORREST: Those people have nothing to do with me!
(FORREST *walks away. Pause*.)
(*Finally*) You want him to stay here.

RYDER: I shouldn't be too long. We can't go back to the hotel.

MACREADY: No.

RYDER: I'll take him to Boston. We have friends. (*Beat*.) He can
get a boat home from there. (*Beat*.) But if you don't want
to . . .

FORREST: He can stay.
(*Short pause*.)

RYDER: He'll need some clothes.

FORREST: He can stay. Don't be long.
(RYDER *hesitates, then hurries out. Pause*.)

MACREADY: He didn't know where else to bring me. Could I have
another?

(*He holds out his glass.*)

FORREST: Listen.

(*Pause. From outside the noise of the mob. After a moment* FORREST *goes and gets the bottle and pours* MACREADY *a drink.*)

FORREST: Were they really shouting my name again?

(MACREADY *nods.*)

What the hell did they think they were doing?

MACREADY: You obviously – . For them. For some of them. Represent – .

(*He shrugs.*)

FORREST: I'm an actor!

(MACREADY *shrugs again. Pause.*)

MACREADY: Any money I do receive I shall give away. I did not perform for . . . (*Beat.*) I'm not a greedy man. (*Beat.*) The charities I support, I should give you a list, I also give anonymously to – .

FORREST: Shut up. (*Short pause.*) Please. Your generosity is well known.

MACREADY: Is it? (*Beat.*) Good.

(MACREADY *looks towards a clothes trunk, hesitates, then goes to look in it.*)

FORREST: Take whatever you need. Whatever might fit. A cape maybe . . .

(*He shrugs. Pause.* MACREADY *begins to look through the costume trunk. From outside closer gunshots, and shouts.*)

(*Suddenly turns to the noise and screams.*) Leave us alone in here!!!!!!

(*Pause.*)

MACREADY: (*Pulling something out of the trunk; quietly*) Is this your Lear?

(FORREST *nods.*)

It's funny how we rarely get a chance to see each other's . . .

FORREST: I've seen your Lear. (*Beat.*) I found the time to see your Lear.

(*Short pause.*)

MACREADY: Is that it? You've just seen it? You don't want to say – ?

93

FORREST: (*Quickly*) I enjoyed it.
(*Short pause.*)
MACREADY: You've got an interesting costume.
FORREST: So did you.
MACREADY: Actually this sort of looks like mine.
(*Short pause.*)
(*Without looking up*) How was *your* play tonight?
FORREST: Fine. (*Laughs to himself.*) There was no riot. A large section of my audience did not try to murder me. The theatre is not burning. Not a bad night. (*Beat.*) They love Metamora, the noble savage. (*Beat.*) Who has the decency to die. (*Smiles.*) So they cheered as always. I was not very good tonight, I thought.
(*He shrugs.*)
MACREADY: As we get older . . . It's funny, isn't it? When we begin – when I began – I thought always about what they would think about me. (*Beat.*) You want so much to please them. (*Beat.*) But you get older – and that's still there – but . . . Well, it's us who start to judge them, isn't it?
FORREST: I'm not that old yet.
(*Short pause.*)
MACREADY: (*Choosing to ignore him*) Sometimes you stand on that stage and know you are achieving a level of excellence few before you have ever achieved. And you watch an audience watching you as if on some river bank staring at the natural flow of water. (*Beat.*) And then on other nights – probably like you felt tonight – you hate what you've done, perhaps even embarrassed – .
FORREST: I didn't say I was – .
MACREADY: And your audience receives you with rapturous attention and applause. (*Beat.*) There seems to be no rhyme or reason. (*Beat.*) The older you get, the more confusing it all becomes. The reaction. Like tonight, what you were telling me about your performance. Where's the logic.
(FORREST *looks at him.*)
And I'll tell you what makes it all even worse. It's going to see another perform – especially a part that you know like your own soul – and then witnessing grotesque exaggeration,

94

which one could forgive perhaps in a novice, but when it's an actor of some note, some ambition. And then when the crowd – the mob, one should call them in this case – greets this fraud with its misplaced adulation, I find myself in an almost state of total fevered despair.

(*Short pause.*)

FORREST: I enjoy watching other actors – .

MACREADY: When they are excellent! Which is so rare, as we both know so well.

(*Short pause.*)

FORREST: I enjoy watching other actors even when they're bad, even when they're silly.

MACREADY: But then when an audience praises – .

FORREST: I enjoyed your Hamlet a great deal. (*Beat.*) When I was in London. I enjoyed it. (*Short pause.*) That dance you did – Hamlet's little dance before the Gertrude scene. I'd never seen anything like it. I will never forget it.

MACREADY: You're not the first to – .

FORREST: A fancy dance? I asked myself. Where does this come from in the play? I knew no reference to it. I had never before seen an actor – .

MACREADY: An expression of his madness. A colour. A texture of the performance.

FORREST: And a costume for this dance which, if I remember correctly, had a dress with a waist up to about the armpits, huge overlarge black gloves – .

MACREADY: True, I – .

FORREST: A great big hat with a gigantic plume – .

MACREADY: The character is mad!

FORREST: Is this Hamlet or Malvolio, I remember saying to myself. But still, I enjoyed it.

(*Suddenly turns to* MACREADY.)

It's true, Hamlet is mad. And in preparation for my own performance I became a student of the mind's disease, visiting asylums and talking not only with the doctors but also with the ill. And the result of this study, Mr Macready, was the knowledge that true madness is expressed through the heart, not the costume. Madness is not funny clothes, but a funny soul.

95

MACREADY: We are different actors.

FORREST: This is very true.

MACREADY: You study asylums and I study the play.

FORREST: That's not – .

MACREADY: Perhaps I am old-fashioned, but I continue to believe that all one needs is to be found in the play. Mr Shakespeare knew what – .

FORREST: I don't disagree.

(*Beat.*)

MACREADY: Then perhaps all I am saying is – from one actor to another – a little more time with the text and a little less in asylums might do a world of good.

FORREST: You haven't even seen – .

MACREADY: One hears, Mr Forrest, one hears! It is a small business we're in.

FORREST: In that case, as we are talking text, perhaps – as one actor to another – I can make a suggestion as I have also seen your Othello.

MACREADY: You *are* a fan, I'm flattered.

FORREST: As I've said, I enjoy watching other actors – whatever they do. Anyway, *Othello*. (*Begins to recite:*)

'Rude am I in my speech,
And little blessed with the soft phrase of peace;
For since these arms of mine had seven years' pith'

(MACREADY *joins in.*)

BOTH: 'Till now some nine moons wasted, they have used
Their dearest action in the tented field;
And little of this great world can I speak
More than pertains to feats of broil and battle;'

(FORREST *drops out.*)

MACREADY: 'And therefore little shall I grace my cause
In speaking for *myself.*'

FORREST: 'For *myself*'! That's just how you said it when I saw you.

MACREADY: And that is the line.

FORREST: That's not the meaning though. (*Laughs.*) Othello starts by saying he is rude in speech, how there is little he can speak about except battles. So what he is saying here is that he's bad at *speaking*, not that he doesn't want to talk or have people talk

96

about him. He's not being humble, for Christ's sake, he's saying that he's awkward and out of place where he is! So the line should be!:

'And therefore little shall I grace my cause
In *speaking* for myself.'
(*Beat.*)

MACREADY: That's a different reading. It's interesting. But it's just a different reading.

FORREST: It's the right reading!

MACREADY: That's your opinion.

FORREST: And when I go and see your Othello again that's how you'll be saying the line, I'm sure. (*Smiles.*) Here, you want another one! The same scene:

'Which I observing,
Took once a pliant hour, and found *good* means
To draw from her a prayer of earnest heart
That I would all my pilgrimage dilate'

And so on. (*Beat.*) '*Good* means'! Not 'Good *means*'!

MACREADY: I don't hear the difference.

FORREST: He was after a *good* reason, a *good* way, a just way to get his promise. As opposed to a successful means to – .
(*From outside sudden gunshots which are closer. Short pause.*)

MACREADY: The other reading maybe. But not this . . .

FORREST: Fine. Fine. At least I got you to agree about one. (*Short pause.*) I only brought it up because – . What you said, about reading the . . .
(*Crowd noise off.* MACREADY *looks through the trunk. Long pause.* MACREADY *pulls out a costume.*)

MACREADY: Richard?
(FORREST *nods.* MACREADY *pulls out an identical costume.*)
Why two?

FORREST: I started with the hump on my left and my left hand curled – . Then I broke my right wrist, so I had to change, put the hump on the right.
(MACREADY *nods.*)
Now I keep them both. I've found that if I've got three or four Richards close together, I switch back and forth. It helps the back.

MACREADY: Kean I think did that too.

FORREST: Did he?

(*Pause.*)

MACREADY: Kemble too. I think. (*Beat.*) Ever see Kemble's . . .
(*Mimics Kemble's walk as Richard III. FORREST laughs.*)
I don't know what it was about him. Every time he tried – .
Hamlet. Richard. Macbeth. (*Beat.*) But did you see his
Cassio?

FORREST: No, I – . No.

MACREADY: Brilliant. (*Beat.*) He was a first-rate actor, but only in
second-rate parts.

FORREST: I've known other – .

MACREADY: An incomparable Cassio. (*Beat.*) You've never
played – .

FORREST: No.

MACREADY: Neither have I. (*Pause.*) There are so many great
supporting parts in Shakespeare. When I was young we'd
fight for them.

FORREST: They still – .

MACREADY: Not in England any more. You used to have to
constantly look over your shoulder. People had ambition!
Now no one wants to work. No one wants to begin. But they
work in my productions. (*Laughs.*) And so they hate me.
(*Laughs.*) You want to know what it's like in London today?
I tried to correct this actor. He works for me. And he's a
nothing. All I say to him is, 'Please do not speak your speech
in that drawling way, sir.' I'm very polite. 'Here,' I tell him,
'speak it like this: "To ransom home revolted Mortimer!"
That's how you speak it!' (*Beat.*) He turns to me, in front of
the whole company, and says, 'I know that, sir – that is the
way, but you'll please remember you get one hundred
pounds a week for speaking it in your way, and I only get
thirty shillings for mine! Give me one hundred pounds and
I'll speak it your way; but I'm not going to do for thirty
shillings what you get paid one hundred pounds for.'
(MACREADY *laughs*, FORREST *smiles.*)
Actors.
(*He shakes his head. Short pause.*)

FORREST: What I hate is when they come late for rehearsal.

MACREADY: Which happens more and – .

FORREST: Once, a rehearsal of mine was being delayed by this
actor; he only had a small part, but it was quite an important
part in the first scene. So we were all waiting. (*Beat*.) I
became visibly upset. Everyone knew enough to stay away
from me. And when finally the truant – a quiet gentlemanly
man, who had never before been late for one second – once
he arrived I knew I needed to make an example of him.
(*Beat. Smiling*) So I said, 'Sir, you have kept these ladies and
gentlemen waiting for a full half hour.'

(MACREADY *nods and smiles*.)

'You cannot be ignorant, sir, of the importance of a rehearsal
in which every member of the company is to take part!'
(*Beat*.) At that moment, this actor looked at me. I could see
there were tears now in his eyes.

(MACREADY *smiles and shakes his head*.)

And then he spoke. 'Mr Forrest, sir,' he said, 'I beg your
pardon. I could not come sooner.'

(FORREST *looks at* MACREADY, *who snickers*.)

'My son – my only son – died last night. I hurried here as
soon as I could.'

(MACREADY *suddenly stops smiling. Short pause.* FORREST
looks at MACREADY *and shakes his head*.)

Actors.

(*Long pause.* MACREADY *goes back and looks into the costume
trunk*.

Slow fade to blackout.)

(*The bare stage of the Broadway Theatre.* MACREADY *and*
FORREST *enter – each having thrown on pieces of different
costumes. As they enter, they are giggling and carrying swords*.)
Who taught you fencing?

MACREADY: Angelo?

(FORREST *shakes his head*.)

You haven't heard of him? He's wonderful. He's dead now.
But he was wonderful when I was young.

(*They are centre stage looking out at the house*.)

99

FORREST: It's paradise. Even without an audience.

MACREADY: Especially without an – .

BOTH: Audience.

(FORREST *tips Macready's sword, he smiles and they begin to fence. After some time:*)

FORREST: Come for a third, Laertes.

MACREADY: I thought *I* was Hamlet.

FORREST: You should have spoken sooner.

(*They fence.*)

    'You but dally.

      I pray you pass with your best violence;

      I am afeard you make a wanton of me.'

MACREADY: I don't know his lines.

FORREST: (*Stops*) You don't know Laertes . . .

MACREADY: I'm never listening at this point. (*Beat.*) What is it?

(FORREST *thought he heard something, but now shakes his head.*)

FORREST: Should we go back into my – ? Ryder shouldn't be much longer.

MACREADY: I don't care.

FORREST: I suppose he will find us here.

MACREADY: (*Looking out*) How many seats?

FORREST: Nine hundred and seventy-eight. (*Beat.*) I added those seats over there.

MACREADY: Can they see – ?

FORREST: No one's complained. I've been waiting for someone to complain, but . . .

(*He shrugs.*)

MACREADY: I wouldn't want to sit there.

FORREST: No.

(MACREADY *walks to the apron to get a closer look, then turns to see the particular sight line. He shakes his head.*)

MACREADY: No, I wouldn't.

FORREST: I do play to them at times. I try to. (*Beat.*) I try to remember to, but they are way over there. Added fifty-three seats.

(MACREADY *suddenly turns, thinks he hears something.*)

FORREST: It's outside.

(MACREADY *nods*.)
I have it for another five weeks. The sound is very good.
Much better than a lot of . . . I hate your theatre.

MACREADY: It's not my . . .

FORREST: They should tear the Astor Place down, if you want my opinion.

MACREADY: That may in fact be being done.

(FORREST *walks to the apron and speaks into the house, at first to show off the acoustics.*)

FORREST: (*As he speaks Othello he gains in passion*)
'It is the cause, it is the cause, my soul.
Let me not name it to you, you chaste stars!
It is the cause. Yet I'll not shed her blood,
Nor scar that whiter skin of hers than snow,
And smooth as monumental alabaster.
Yet she must die, else she'll betray more men.
Put out the light, and then put out the light.

(*He chokes up.*)
If I quench thee, thou flaming minister,
I can again thy former light restore,
Should I repent me; but once put out thy light,
Thou cunning'st pattern of excelling nature,
I know not where is that Promethean heat
That can thy light relume. When I have plucked the rose,
I cannot give it vital growth again;
It needs must wither. I'll smell thee on the tree . . .'

(*He cannot go on. He covers his face, hiding his tears. Pause.*)

MACREADY: (*Without looking at him*) You should add a few *Othellos* next week. (*Beat.*) I'm sorry about your wife leaving.

(FORREST *turns to him. Short pause.*)

Play it out. (*Beat.*) You are certainly right about the sound.

FORREST: Go ahead and . . . (*He tries to get a hold of himself.*) Really, go ahead . . .

(*Short pause.* MACREADY *walks to the apron.*)

MACREADY: You'll be hard to follow.

FORREST: Modesty? You're acting already, Mr Macready. And acting well.

(*He smiles,* MACREADY *turns to the house.*)

MACREADY: 'Rumble thy bellyful. Spit, fire. Spout, rain.
    Nor rain, wind, thunder, fire are my daughters.
    I tax not you, you elements – .
    (*From outside, quite near, gunfire and shouts.*)
FORREST: (*Screams*) I told you before, to just leave us alone!!!!!
    (*Pause.*)
MACREADY: (*Continues*)
                you elements, with unkindness.
    I never gave you kingdom, called you children;
    You owe me no subscription. Then let fall
    Your horrible pleasure. Here I stand your slave,
    A poor, infirm, weak, and despised old man.'
    (*He stops. Continues to stare out.* RYDER *has entered upstage, he carries a cape. Pause.*)
RYDER: Mr Macready?
FORREST: (*Turns without seeing who it is*) Leave us in peace!!!
    (MACREADY *turns,* FORREST *sees who it is.*)
RYDER: I have the horses. (*Beat.*) We must go. Put on this. (*Goes to give him the cape.*) Why are you dressed like . . . ?
    (MACREADY *looks at* FORREST.)
FORREST: We were rehearsing – .
RYDER: Rehearsing – ?
MACREADY: Give me the cape. What's it like out there?
RYDER: It's gotten worse. (*Beat.*) Reports are that there are
    nearly thirty-five people now dead. And hundreds seriously
    . . . (*Beat.*) Hundreds wounded.
    (*Beat.*)
    We should hurry. There are people who are running through
    the streets looking for that English actor 'Macreilly or
    whatever his name is'. (*Beat.*) Buses have been stopped,
    turned on their side and set afire, on just the rumour that you
    were aboard. (*Beat.*) Our hotel – . I had to go past. That too
    has been torched.
FORREST: Go.
RYDER: Put up the hood.
    (RYDER *pulls up the hood of the cape on* MACREADY.)
    We have a safe house for tonight in New Rochelle. We'll go

to Boston in the morning. Come on.

(*As they start to leave,* MACREADY *stops and looks back at the theatre.*)

There's talk that they'll close the theatres.

(*Pause.*)

MACREADY: You should come to England again, Mr Forrest.

(*Beat.*) And get away from all these troubles.

(*Short pause.*)

FORREST: I'm away from all these troubles here.

(MACREADY *nods and leaves with* RYDER. *Pause.* FORREST *starts to go, stops and comes back. He looks around the theatre. With sword in hand, he stands, not knowing where else on earth he wants to go.*)

THE END